Practice & Improve Your

FRENCH

The Handbook

Chantal Marsden

PASSPORT BOOKS
a division of *NTC Publishing Group*
Lincolnwood, Illinois USA

Note
All the characters and incidents in this book and the accompanying recorded material are fictitious and bear no relation to any known person, firm or company.

Handbook written by:
Chantal Marsden

Chantal Marsden, the author of this course, has taught English in Paris and is now a freelance translator and writer.

Package Photo Credits
Front cover: top left, middle left, bottom left—French Government Tourist Office; bottom right, top right—Air France
Back cover: Susan Locke

This edition first published in 1988 by Passport Books, a division of
NTC Publishing Group, 4255 West Touhy Avenue,
Lincolnwood, Illinois 60646-1975 U.S.A.
Developed by Harrap Limited.
©Harrap Limited, 1986. All rights reserved.
No part of this book may be reproduced, stored in a retrieval
system, or transmitted in any form, or by any means,
electronic, mechanical, photocopying or otherwise, without the
prior permission of NTC Publishing Group.
Manufactured in the United States of America.

8 9 0 ML 9 8 7 6 5 4 3 2 1

CONTENTS

CONTENTS OF APPENDICES

About the
"Practice & Improve" series

Passport Books' "Practice & Improve" series represents a new kind of approach to learning languages. The idea is to mirror as closely as possible the experience of living in a foreign country and hearing the language spoken in natural, day-to-day conversations. The cassettes are designed for relaxed listening on a car stereo or a Walkman, so you can play them while you are traveling to work, going to school, doing housework and so on.

The story

Each course consists of a combination of drama and practice materials interspersed with music. The dramatic scenes build into a story − rather similar to a radio play. The recordings are all in stereo and include realistic sound effects which serve both to create the atmosphere and to give important clues about what is happening.

All recorded material is in the target language. The script has been carefully constructed to allow for the emphasis and repetition of important elements. Otherwise, however, the conversation that you will hear is completely authentic, and deliberately includes all the hesitations and interjections of normal speech.

The course is intended for entertaining and *repeated* listening. It is therefore not necessary for you to try and understand every word right away. The important thing, particularly if you have only a basic knowledge of your chosen language, is to be patient: don't become obsessed with details. Each time you listen you will understand more − words and phrases will become increasingly familiar and will start to stick in your mind.

The practices

The practice sections highlight particular language points that occur in the preceding or following scene of the story. They allow you to review the basic elements of structure and grammar while concentrating on the language you are likely to need when traveling or working abroad. You can join in with the practices if you want, or simply think the answers to yourself — it's up to you. Most sections have a gentle background music accompaniment; this is to promote a relaxed response and, at a more subliminal level, to aid your retention of the language.

Accent

The practices are spoken by actors whose native accent is, as far as possible, a neutral and agreed standard for the language being learned. They provide the models for your pronunciation.

Within the story, on the other hand, different regional accents are present in order to familiarize you with the varying pronunciations you are likely to encounter when traveling through different areas or countries.

The Guide

The story and the practices are explained and commented on by a "Guide", who provides the continuity between the different sections and effectively replaces the headings and instructions you find in conventional language courses.

The Guide and Handbook

The Guide provides an exact transcript of the words spoken on tape. If you have problems understanding a particular word or phrase, you can look it up in the Guide and then refer to the appropriate section in the Handbook or to a dictionary.

The Handbook is provided as a source of reference and instruction. It contains summaries of the scenes and practices as well as notes, appendices and wordlists. (The wordlists, by the way, are not intended to be exhaustive: they cover only the less common words in the language.)

Remember that these books are not intended to be studied in a formal way. They are to prime and prompt you for your main activity − listening.

Level

It is important to bear in mind that "Practice & Improve" is *not an introductory course*. It will not be suitable for you if you have no previous knowledge of the language you are studying. However, if you have a basic background–from learning in school or taking a beginner's course–you'll find the approach ideal, positively refreshing.

The two courses available are set up in order of difficulty. "Practice & Improve Your French" gives more review of the basic points of grammar at an early stage. If you are a bit rusty on the basics, you'll find you need that course. However, if you are already confident of your grasp of the grammar and ground rules, you can go straight into "Practice & Improve Your French PLUS," if you wish: there's no need to work through the first course.

The level you achieve will depend largely on your own aptitude and application. The courses offer you the chance to become fluent in your chosen language, given time and practice. If, on the other hand, you are studying for a particular purpose — an oral exam, a business trip or a holiday, for instance — you can make great progress simply by listening through and concentrating on the particular situations and areas of language that interest you. The courses are designed for complete flexibility: the end product of learning is ultimately dependent on your own requirements and motivation.

How to Study

A relaxed approach

The most important thing is to be relaxed. Part of the
philosophy underlying the course is based on the increased
learning efficiency achieved by *not* concentrating too hard on
the material you are studying. This is why "Practice & Improve" is ideal for listening to while you are engaged in some
other task.

First things first

Following these instructions there is a brief outline of the main
features of the target language − its similarities to and
differences from English. If your knowledge is very rusty, you
might like to read through this to refresh your memory. If you
have difficulty with any of the descriptive terms used, there is
a short glossary at the back of the book to help you.

Using the course

The best approach is to read through the summaries of the
scenes and practices for the tape you are going to listen to.
These summaries are contained at the top of every other page
in this Handbook. It shouldn't take you long to look through
them−but don't try to do too much at once: one side of a cassette at a time will be sufficient.

Now you are ready to listen to the tape. Play one side all the
way through while the summaries are fresh in your mind.

Listen through again. This time you can join in with the practice sections if you wish and rewind the cassette selectively to listen to certain sections again. You can keep repeating this process as often as you like and, as you do so, you will find that you will become more and more at ease with the language you hear. You will soon begin to anticipate words and phrases, rather like picking up the lyrics of a song: this is excellent – it means that you are starting to *think* in the language.

As you listen through, you will also find that sections which appeared difficult to understand will gradually become clear to you as the context surrounding them becomes more familiar. You can, of course, aid this process by referring to the wordlists, notes and appendices in the Handbook. But (unless you are completely lost) don't do this at too early a stage: it's important not to become obsessed by details of grammar and meaning before you have given yourself a chance to "discover" the language. Your learning and retention will be much better if it comes as a result of absorbing the target language rather than as a response to a lot of rules and translations in your own language.

Take it easy!

The process described applies to each cassette, of course. Don't try to rush it: give each cassette side a "fair hearing" before going on to the next. However, you shouldn't take this to extremes. If you start to become bored with a cassette, you should immediately go on to the next one.

Enjoyment is important

These recommendations are designed to help you get the most out of "Practice & Improve your French". Ultimately, of course, the way to study the materials is up to you. You may find it impossible to break the habit of a lifetime, and find yourself sitting down at a desk with the Listening Guide and Handbook as you listen to the cassettes. If you are happier this way, then that is the best approach to adopt. Above all, you should make sure you enjoy the activity of language learning.

Just bear in mind that much of the research into language learning indicates that a relaxed attitude pays dividends and that the idea of learning a language structure by structure is *not* the most effective strategy. The development of familiarity with a new language can be seen more as the process of an artist gradually filling in the details of a canvas than as an analogy with, shall we say, bricklaying.

The French Language

As has already been pointed out, this course is not really intended for complete beginners, and it is therefore likely that you, the student, already have some knowledge of the language, however small or however long ago you may have acquired it. These notes, therefore, are just intended to refresh your memory and to make you more aware of various important features of the language.

Gender

All French nouns fall into two categories: masculine and feminine. The grammatical distinction between these two genders is often indicated by the presence of the definite or indefinite article **(le/la, les; un/une, des)** in front of the noun. However, the distinction is also carried through to all the words used to qualify or refer back to the noun. For instance: **la maison** is a feminine word, so any article, adjective, or Past Participle if the verb is conjugated with **être,** must be in the feminine too:

la grande maison   **la maison est habitée**
une jolie maison   **les maisons ont été agrandies,** etc.

And, if we wish to refer back to **la maison,** we would do so using the pronoun **elle** because, effectively, French has no equivalent of the neutral word "it". All this sometimes appears rather frustrating and pointless to English-speakers, particularly because there is no obvious reason why a particular noun should be masculine or feminine. However, it is a feature that you must come to terms with, and one of the best ways of doing so is to try and memorize a noun together with its article at the outset: **le bureau, la ville** etc. You will soon find that this pays dividends and that the procedure of agreements then becomes automatic. One final point on this subject: don't become obsessed by correctness – the use of the wrong gender is not usually a bar to successful communication.

Familiar (tu) and polite (vous) forms

This point can cause a few uncertainties at first, mainly as to when, addressing whom, **tu** should be used. There are a few simple, reliable guidelines one can give on this: **tu** is used when addressing family, close friends and small children. In other cases one should use **vous,** and it is safe to say that, if in doubt, **vous** is the one to use. This being said, do not be surprised if you hear people addressing each other as **tu** when they have just met, especially young people. The trend is towards much less formality nowadays, and most young people use **tu** straight away on meeting for the first time. Older people tend to use **vous** to start with, and the passage to the **tu** form **(le tutoiement)** is usually an indication that people like each other and are becoming more than just colleagues or acquaintances: close friends. The ritual question asked when someone wishes to start addressing another person as **tu** is: **Vous permettez que je vous tutoie?,** or **Je peux vous tutoyer/vous dire tu?,** or **On pourrait peut-être se dire tu?**

Verb endings

These are on the whole more complex and varied in French than they are in English. An obvious example of this is the verb **aller,** as compared to the verb *to go:* **je vais, tu vas, il va, nous allons, vous allez, ils vont,** as against: *I go, you go, he goes, we go, you go, they go.* Each verb tense distinguishes person and number in this way – by the use of different endings. These endings are set out in the Appendix at the back of the book. This is one area where a little parrot-fashion learning may come in useful: verb endings are critical to understanding and making yourself understood. A little time spent learning the most frequently used tenses will help you communicate much more fluently.

Verb tenses

These are used slightly differently in French and English, and for once one can say that English is more complex, more difficult (to a dispassionate observer, if there is such a thing!), than French.

SIMPLE AND CONTINUOUS

The Present tense in French only ever consists of one word, and corresponds to both the Simple and the Continuous Present tense in English: **je vais** means both *I go* and *I am going,* **je mange:** *I eat* and *I am eating,* etc. The same pattern applies to other tenses: **je mangeais** can mean *I ate, I was eating, I used to eat, I would eat* – in the sense of *I used to ...* (To emphasize the idea of a continuous action, however, you will notice that the French often use the expression **être en train de** + Infinitive.)

PAST TENSES

French has several tenses for relating past events. The most frequently used is the Perfect tense (**Passé Composé**), which corresponds to both the Past Simple and Present Perfect tenses in English:

English	French
Did you write a letter?	**Tu as/Vous avez écrit une**
Have you written a letter?	**lettre?**
I sent a telex and I phoned the director.	**J'ai envoyé un télex et**
I have sent a telex and phoned the director.	**téléphoné au directeur.**

For descriptions and states – as opposed to completed actions – the Imperfect tense is usually used when talking about the past. As you listen to the course, the conventions of which tense to use in what circumstances will become much clearer to you – both through numerous examples and through the notes.

FUTURE TENSES

English and French share quite a lot of common ground in their use of Future tenses. Both languages have a "going to" future of intention, as well as a simple "shall/will" form. The French also use the Present tense quite frequently when they wish to refer to an action that is to happen in the near future. In many ways this is similar to the English use of the Present Continuous in situations such as: "I'm leaving in five minutes" or "I'm meeting him today."

One area of particular difficulty for English speakers, however, is the use of Future tenses after **quand** *(when):* **Quand il finira son travail ...** *(When he finishes his work ...).* This is a convention which takes some getting used to, especially if, as many learners do, you tend to think in English when trying to speak French. That is why we emphasize the importance of relaxed and repeated listening: it is much more effective to absorb examples of different linguistic conventions than to try and follow them as abstract rules of translation when trying to speak.

DURATION

The above comments also apply to the use of tenses with **depuis** *(for, since).* It seems strange, for example, to English ears that a French speaker should express the idea *I have lived here for three years* by using the Present tense: **J'habite ici depuis trois ans.** To the French, however, using a Past tense would change the meaning completely, leading the listener to assume that the action was over.

INFINITIVE

Another feature of French which differs quite markedly from English is its use of the Infinitive (the "to" form of the verb). The Infinitive is very often used in French where the verb form in *-ing* would be used in English. For instance:

English	French
I like dancing.	**J'aime danser.**
	Comprendre les Français n'est pas facile.
Understanding French people is not easy.	**Il n'est pas facile de comprendre les Français.**

THE SUBJUNCTIVE

The Subjunctive is something of a stumbling block for many learners of French – especially those who have studied at school. It is particularly difficult for English speakers because there is not really a direct equivalent in our language.
It is important to remember, however, that at a basic level of speaking the use of the Subjunctive is not essential for successful communication. It is something that you will pick up gradually:

you will become accustomed to using it after certain verbs and structures.

Generally speaking, the Subjunctive is used when referring to a situation or action that exists in the realms of possibility or probability rather than reality. Once again, however, it is important to be aware of and absorb the examples which occur in the course. These are frequently pointed out in the notes in this Handbook – giving you plenty of opportunity to become familiar with both the forms and usage of the Subjunctive "mood".

Articles, definite (le, la, les) and indefinite (un, une, des)

The use of articles differs significantly between English and French. This point is brought out more fully in both the notes and the Appendix. In several instances one can, in fact, say that the way in which articles are used in French is the opposite of that in English. For example, the definite article is usually placed before abstract nouns; on the other hand, it is not necessary to place the indefinite article before names of professions: **Je suis médecin.** *(I am a doctor.)*

Stress on a word or group of words in the sentence

This is a point which you will find mentioned many times throughout the notes. It is interesting to hear how, in French, the emphasis is put on a word/group of words in a sentence by using a particular expression or word order, whereas in English this is done simply by stressing the relevant word or group orally. For instance:

Did you call me?   **C'est toi qui m'as appelé?**

I want that dress!   **C'est cette robe-là** que je veux!, etc.

Pronunciation

This is an area where *most* things are completely different from your own language, so perhaps it will help if we try to list briefly here the main differences and to examine the way in which French sounds function.

VOWEL SOUNDS

The main thing to be aware of is that French vowel sounds should be short, clear-cut sounds, not diphthongs – that is to say you should not linger on them when you say them. It will take you quite a long time to achieve the right sound, as this is quite a subtle area of pronunciation. Being conscious at this stage of what you should aim for should help you to improve as you listen to the course. This general point having been made, the following points are worth watching out for in particular:

u AS DISTINCT FROM ou

u is a sound which does not exist at all in English and therefore one of the most difficult to get absolutely right. Here, practice will eventually make perfect. The following list contains words with both **u** and **ou** sounds. Listen for them when you study the course.

u	ou
rue	route
du	douce
sur	sous
lune	lourd

e/é/è

Your natural tendency here will be to pronounce the **e** as **é** when placed in the first syllable of a word, whereas it should be pronounced as a neutral **e,** without any accent. Practising the following words should help:

> **premier**
> **regarde**
> **mener**
> **lever**
> **remercier**

You will also notice that French people very often drop the **e** sound when it occurs in a weak position in a word or sentence. Again, this is quite a subtle point of pronunciation, but being aware of it should help you to reproduce the right sound.

THE eu SOUND

This is a sound between **u** and **e,** and there are two ways
of pronouncing it: "open" as in **heure,** and "closed" as in **deux.**
Listen carefully for the difference when you play the
recordings, and practise saying the following words when you
have a minute. It should help you get these sounds right:

open **eu**	closed **eu**
heure	**deux**
bonheur	**bleu**
malheur	**cheveux**
peur	**heureux**
sœur	**affreux**

THE TWO o SOUNDS: OPEN AS IN **Rome,** CLOSED AS IN **trop**

The following are common words which you can practise saying
alternately once you have listened to the recordings. Practise in
particular the **or** group, in which the **o** has got to be open,
otherwise the **r** cannot be pronounced:

open **o/or**	closed **o**
porte	**mot**
encore	**trop**
morte	**dos**
Rome	**eau**
col	**gros**
Paul	**faux**

CONSONANTS

The main feature here is that most final consonants in French
words are not pronounced. There are a few exceptions to this,
such as **mars, fils, sept, net,** for instance, but mostly the
consonants placed at the end of a word are silent. For example
(silent consonants are in bold italics):

cor*ps,* taba*c,* fran*c,* dan*s,* tro*p*

Remember that the -ent verb ending is also silent:

ils aime*nt,* elles parle*nt,* etc.

Some consonants might give you a little more
trouble than others:

r is usually quite a difficult sound to get right for English speakers. The tip of your tongue should be placed downwards (check: if it is placed upwards against your palate, a very English **r** will come out!), behind your lower teeth. This will give you a better chance of reproducing the characteristic guttural, throaty sound of the French **r**.

h is, of course, not pronounced in French: **l'homme, l'hôtel, l'huile,** etc.

s can be pronounced in two different ways:
as **ss,** for instance in:

assis, poisson, Pascale, assez, Marseille, penser
as **z,** between two vowels, for instance in:

mauvaise, poison, Tunisie, peser, chose, chaise

NASAL SOUNDS

These characteristically French sounds are formed by the combination of a vowel and a consonant, **n** or **m.** The result is called a "nasal" sound simply because it is pronounced slightly "through the nose". The nasal sounds are:

a + n/m	an, am	**danse, banlieu/jambe, ambulance**
e + n/m	en, em	**en, pense/novembre, tremble**
i + n/m	in, im	**cinq, vingt/impatient, timbre**
o + n/m	on, om	**bon, allons/tombe, sombre**
u + n	un	**un, lundi, brun**
ai + n	ain	**main, demain, train**

In all these sounds, the **n** and **m** are pronounced together with the vowel as one sound, and are never heard as individual letters.

Stress on syllables and intonation

STRESS

French is not a language which has fixed, stressed syllables like English. The stress in a French word is shared evenly between all syllables, and the mid-syllable in a French word is never stressed. If any syllable is going to be stressed at all, it is the last one, but very slightly. The stress pattern is probably one of the last traces of an English accent to go because it is such a natural, unconscious phenomenon. But, again, it should help to be aware of the difference, and to know what you are aiming for. Compare for instance:

English		French	
e*nor*mously	stressed syllables	**énormément**	no one syllable
mag*ni*ficent	in italics	**magnifique**	bearing the stress

INTONATION

The main difference between French and English intonation is probably a difference in intensity, as you will soon realise when listening to the recordings. This is particularly obvious when people are asking a question: in French the voice must rise clearly at the end of the sentence, whereas it does not always do so in English. Again, intonation is such an unconscious process in your own language that it will take you quite a long time, even after you have mastered the main rules of French pronunciation, to get the intonation in your French sentences absolutely right and natural. Be aware of how the intonation works when you listen to French, and try to reproduce it as best you can, in particular in the oral exercises.

TRIP TO GENEVA

Cassette 1   Side 1
A beautiful day

SCENE 1: Strasbourg – in Pierre's car and in the CGE offices

Pierre is giving one of his colleagues a lift to the office. Having driven through heavy traffic, they arrive at CGE and Pierre's colleague gets out of the car and thanks him. Pierre drives off to leave his car in the office car park. As he enters the office, Pierre greets various people. One of his colleagues, François, asks Pierre's advice about a translation he wants done. Pierre recommends an agency but tells François he'll give him the details later. He has to do everything himself at the moment because Pascale, his secretary, is on holiday.

LANGUAGE NOTES

1 **Il fait beau**
Note the use of the verb **faire** to describe the weather, here followed by the adjective in the masculine. Other ways of saying this appear in the text: **c'est une belle journée** and **il y a du soleil.**

aimer/changer/arriver/déposer/travailler/accompagner/ regarder/donner/utiliser/demander
All these verbs appear in this scene. You will find, in the Grammatical Appendix at the back of the book, a section on verbs listing all the verbs appearing in this Course and the main characteristics, tenses and endings of each verb group. You can refer to this section whenever you come across a new verb in a scene or exercise, and check on its various forms.

Où est-ce que je vous dépose?/Comment vas-tu?
You probably already know that French people address each other as **tu** or **vous** according to whether they know each other well or not. Basically, **tu** is used when addressing members of one's family, close friends or children; **vous** is used with people one does not know very well.

tu as un moment?/C'est une simple traduction?/Tu connais leur numéro?
The easiest and most widely used way of asking a simple question in everyday conversation is to keep the same word order as for a statement and to raise one's voice at the end of the sentence.

ça va?/Comment vas-tu?/Ça va très bien, merci.
These are the most common forms of greeting in French. **Salut** is a familiar, informal greeting, widely used especially among young people.

Il me la faut/je dois l'avoir/Ça ne me déplaît pas
La, l' and **me** are pronouns, which replace nouns previously mentioned and are placed before the verb they refer to. In the above examples, **l'** and **la** are direct pronouns, **me** is an indirect one, meaning **à moi** *(to me)*. But the same pronoun can be both direct and indirect depending how it is used. You will find a full table of these pronouns, with their position in the sentence, in the Appendix at the end of this handbook.

51 **En général, nous, on utilise l'agence Garrault**
On is used all the time instead of **nous** in everyday spoken French. It is followed by a verb in the 3rd person singular. **Nous** is used here to reinforce **on**.

VOCABULARY

la journée	day
en retard	late
presque	almost
agréable	pleasant
déposer	to set down, drop off (a person)
je vous dépose?	can I drop you off?
aller	to go, *here:* to suit
ça vous va?	is that OK?
salut	hello! hi!
tout de suite	right away
avoir l'air	to look
tu as l'air en forme	you look fit
pouvoir	can, to be able
je peux	I can
ce, cette (*m.f.*)	this
la publicité	advertisement
falloir	to be necessary
il me la faut	I need it, I must have it
contenir	to contain
elle contient	it contains
connaître	to know
tu en connais une bonne?	do you know a good one?
utiliser	to use
par cœur	by heart
quelque part	somewhere
devoir	to have to, must
je dois	I must
quelqu'un	somebody
tout seul	alone, on your own
déplaire	to displease
ça ne me déplaît pas	I don't mind, I like it
avoir besoin de	to need
j'(en) ai besoin	I need (them)

EXERCISE 1: Greetings

Before you try to respond in the pauses provided, listen to the whole exercise carefully, using the pauses to think about what you will say. Then do the exercise as many times as you feel necessary.

LANGUAGE NOTES

Je ne suis pas français/... ni belge ... ni suisse
Remember that adjectives indicating nationality do not take a capital letter in French.

10 **Je parle un peu le français**
Note the use of the article **le** here, and again the use of a small **f** in **français,** to signify *the French language.*

VOCABULARY

les salutations	greetings
bienvenue	welcome
le volant	steering-wheel
les enregistrements	recordings
écouter	to listen to
réécoutez-les	listen to them again
souvent	often
permettre	to allow
apprendre	to learn
vous apprendrez	you will learn
de mieux en mieux	better and better
quant à	as for
encore une fois	once again
quelqu'un	somebody
facile	easy
comment allez-vous?	how are you?
ça va	I'm fine

SCENE 2: Strasbourg – in the CGE offices

A woman is looking for Pierre and trying to find out where his office is. In the process, she finds a workman busy emptying out the contents of room 215, which she thinks is Pierre's room. She tries to find out more from the workman: why he is doing this, where Pierre's new office is likely to be, but with little success. The workman invariably answers her queries saying he has no idea, he doesn't know, it's not his problem. A perfect example of a very frustrating conversation, and of the many ways there are in French of saying nothing!

LANGUAGE NOTES

5 **C'est bien son bureau?**
Bien is used here to emphasize the question and seek confirmation of a fact.

Ah ça, j'sais pas/J'en sais rien/j'ai aucune idée
All these are examples of a very colloquial way of speaking. In each of them the **ne** of the negation has been dropped; the full forms would be, of course, **Je ne sais pas, Je n'en sais rien, Je n'ai aucune idée.** This is done all the time in conversation. Note the use of **ne ... aucune,** meaning *not one, not a single one.* **Aucun** is an adjective and agrees with the noun which follows it.

22 **Il n'y a personne**
Note these negatives: **ne** + verb + **personne**
   ne + verb + **rien**
   ne + verb + **aucune,** etc.
Catherine uses the full form of the negative. The workman would probably have said: **Y a personne,** dropping **il** and **ne.**

33 **On me dit de sortir les choses**
In Scene 1, we saw **on** meaning **nous.** Here, it means *they, people.* **On** is very often used in French in instances where the passive form (here: *I am told to ...*) would be used in English.

35 où les mettez-vous?
On the whole Catherine speaks very correct, sometimes slightly formal French. Here she uses the more formal way of asking a question, with the verb put in front: **mettez-vous?** **Les** comes before the verb here, as in a statement.

40 Pas de quoi
This is the alternative polite answer to **merci,** the other one being of course **de rien.**

VOCABULARY

un ouvrier	workman
chercher	to look for
croire	to think, believe
je crois	I think
savoir	to know
j'sais	I know
faire	to do
vous faites	you are doing
vider	to empty
enlever	to remove
laisser	to leave
sortir	to take out
comme d'habitude	as usual
emménager	to move into
aucun, aucune (*m.f.*)	no, not any
aucune idée	no idea
le couloir	corridor
pas de quoi	it's a pleasure, don't mention it

EXERCISE 2: Spelling (1)

It is very important that you should be able to spell words
fluently in French, as it is a skill which one often has to use
in "real life". Listen to the exercise carefully, then try and
do it yourself, checking your spelling, as well as your
pronunciation of the letters against the answers given.

LANGUAGE NOTES

2 **... je saurais**
This is the Present Conditional form of the verb **savoir.**
You will find the forms of the Conditional in the
Grammatical Appendix at the back of this book.

21 **J'ai compris**
The verb **comprendre** (irregular) is here in the Perfect
tense, called **Passé Composé** in French. It is the past
tense most often used, especially in spoken French. You
will find in the Appendix a list of verbs with their Past
Participle which also tells you for each verb whether it is
conjugated with **avoir** or **être** in the Past tense.

21 **Je vais m'exercer**
The main verb here is **s'exercer.** Such verbs, which include
the reflexive pronoun **se (s')** in their Infinitive form
(corresponding to the English form of the verb with *to*),
are called reflexive verbs. There is a form of the
reflexive pronoun corresponding to each personal subject-
pronoun.

VOCABULARY

épeler	to spell
tout haut	aloud
essayer (de)	to try (to)
une majuscule	a capital letter
une cédille	a cedilla
s'exercer	to practise

SCENE 3: Strasbourg – in the CGE offices

Pierre and Catherine meet for the first time. She realises fairly quickly who he is, but he thinks she is a temp. She starts explaining why she is there, but when Pierre invites her to continue the conversation in his office, she has to tell him that he no longer has an office. Just as she is about to explain it all to him, the phone rings: it is François, about that translation ...

LANGUAGE NOTES

5 **je ne l'ai pas vu**
Note the word order when a pronoun is used with the Perfect tense. It comes before the auxiliary verb.

6 **Je crois que c'est là ...**
The phrase **je crois que ...** is used in French as often as *I think* is used in English. Note that in French you cannot leave **que** out of the sentence.

C'est là qu'elle le range/Ça, au moins, c'est une bonne nouvelle
Here are examples of the way in which one stresses a word or group of words in French: **C'est ...que, Ça, c'est ...**
In English, it would be enough to say THAT'S *where she keeps it*/At least, THAT'S *good news,* just stressing the one word when speaking. It is not possible to do this in French. Another instance of this in this scene is in *Le projet de Genève,* **ça vous dit quelque chose?** This type of sentence, where a word or group of words is picked up and reinforced by **ça,** is very frequent in spoken French.

14 **Et vous, vous êtes**
The first **vous** is the emphatic form of the pronoun, used to insist on the subject of the verb: *And YOU are ...*

VOCABULARY

un carnet d'adresses	address book
ranger	to keep, to put away
venir de	to have just
je viens d'arriver	I have just arrived
en congé	on holiday
au moins	at least
une bonne nouvelle	good news
plaisanter	to joke
une secrétaire intérimaire	temp, temporary secretary
ne vous dit rien	doesn't mean anything to you
il s'agit de	it's about
c'est de ça qu'il s'agit	that's what it's about
en train de	in the process of
tout	everything

EXERCISE 3: Numbers

You will find a list of numbers in the Appendix. Listen to the exercise and repeat carefully. Pay attention to the pronunciation of these numbers, and to which letters are sounded (in the words **six, dix, sept, vingt-deux,** etc). Also to the vowel sounds (for instance in **neuf, quatorze, deux**).

LANGUAGE NOTES

There aren't any new structures in this exercise. If you are not sure about the numbers you hear on the recording, refer to the Grammatical Appendix at the back of the book, where you will find a section on numbers.

VOCABULARY

réentendre	hear again
le mien, la mienne (*m.f.*)	mine

SCENE 4: Strasbourg – in the CGE offices

We find Pierre and Catherine where we left them: he is just finishing talking to François on the phone, she is still trying to explain to him what has happened to all the things which were in his office. Pierre is getting more and more agitated, and what bothers him most seems to be the disappearance of his own (not the firm's!) coffee maker. Catherine suggests talking to the supervisor, which Pierre decides to do straight away, asking Catherine to wait for him. She says she can't as all this is likely to take a long time. In the end, they agree to meet again, at 4 o'clock in the afternoon.

LANGUAGE NOTES

1 **essaye l'une ou l'autre**
This is the familiar form of the Imperative, corresponding to the **tu** form of the verb. It is in fact the **tu** form of the verb in the Present tense, with the s at the end omitted for the **-er** verbs (see the section on verbs at the back of the book).

5 **Allons dans mon bureau**
Here we have the **nous** form of the Imperative, which corresponds to the English *Let's* ... It is simply the first person plural of the verb in the Present tense: **allons, disons, chantons, partons,** etc.

Qu'est-ce que c'est que ça?/Mais enfin, qu'est-ce qui se passe?
The addition of **que ça?** in the first sentence, and of **Mais enfin** in the second, indicates at the same time surprise and disapproval, if not indignation.

15 **Il était en train de tout sortir**
This is the way of indicating that something is being done, is taking place: **en train de** + verb in the Infinitive.

26 **ça ira mal**
This is a familiar, colloquial expression meaning *there will be trouble*. Note in passing the very, very irregular Future tense of the verb **aller**.

Disons vers quatre heures/D'accord
Note these useful expressions to suggest an arrangement
and agree to it.

71 **A tout à l'heure**
This is the form of farewell used when one is likely to see
someone again very shortly.

VOCABULARY

mes affaires (*f.*)	my things
se passer	to happen
qu'est-ce qui se passe?	what's happening?
tout à l'heure	in a moment
c'est un peu fort	that's going a bit far
prévenir	to warn
sans prévenir	without any warning, notice
une cafetière	coffee maker
appartenir (à)	to belong (to)
elle n'appartient pas	it doesn't belong
une société	company
attendre	to wait
vraiment	really
régler	to sort out
le temps que je règle	until I sort out
cette histoire	this business, problem
j'ai pris mes dispositions	I've arranged
revenir	to come back
ça vous convient?	is that convenient?
à tout à l'heure	see you in a moment, later

EXERCISE 4: Confirming and denying

There are many ways of indicating that one is agreeing or disagreeing in French. Here are a few, for you to practise.

LANGUAGE NOTES

2 **Je sais ce qu'il ressent** *I know how he feels*
literally: *I know what he feels.*

3 **j'aimerais**
This is the form used to formulate a polite request. An alternative would be **Je voudrais.** Both verbs are followed by a verb in the Infinitive: **J'aimerais réentendre/ Je voudrais bien le savoir.**

18 **Vous, vous êtes ...**
Another instance of how to insist on a word in French: here, one pronoun is used to emphasize the other. Compare with the English: *And YOU are ...*

Je ne suis pas secrétaire/Vous êtes intérimaire
No article before names of professions in French when stating what someone's profession is.

38 **je me suis trompé**
You remember that reflexive verbs (such as **se tromper**) take **être** in the Past tense.

VOCABULARY

contredire	to contradict
ressentir	to feel
je sais ce qu'il ressent	I know how he feels
avoir raison	to be right
quelqu'un a raison	somebody's right
avoir tort	to be wrong
deviner	to guess
pas du tout	not at all
se tromper	to make a mistake
je me suis trompé(e)	I've made a mistake

SCENE 5: Strasbourg – in the CGE offices

At the beginning of the scene Catherine is with the director, who congratulates her on having been chosen for the Geneva assignment. She thanks him for all the help he's given her. She explains she has to leave him to go and see Pierre. We find her again in Pierre's office. He apologizes for his hurried departure in the morning, and proceeds to ask her what her name is … They are just beginning to understand each other when they are rudely interrupted by our old friend the workman, who is determined to move Pierre's things into his new office then and there. He won't listen to Catherine and Pierre's protests, so the unhappy pair have to go in search of another office in which to continue their fascinating conversation.

LANGUAGE NOTES

Pas de tout./Je vous en prie./Je n'y manquerai pas.
Note all these polite acknowledgements of thanks, offers of help, etc.

7 **Ils doivent vous estimer beaucoup**
Here **devoir** indicates a very strong probability: *they must hold you in very high esteem.*

Il faut que je voie Pierre./Il est temps que je parte.
Voie and **parte** are forms of the verbs **voir** and **partir** in the Subjunctive. Quite a number of set phrases are followed by the Subjunctive, and you will find its different forms and endings listed in the list of verbs at the back of the book.

Il est plus de quatre heures/Je pars à quatre heures et demie./il est quatre heures passées.
There are several mentions of the time in this scene, so here is a good opportunity to practise telling the time. Refresh your memory with the following examples:

Quelle heure est-il?

Il est quatre heures.	*(It's four o'clock.)*
Il est quatre heures et quart.	*(It's quarter past four.)*
Il est quatre heures vingt-cinq.	*(It's twenty-five past four.)*
Il est quatre heures et demie.	*(It's half past four.)*
Il est cinq heures moins vingt-cinq.	*(It's twenty-five to five.)*
Il est cinq heures moins le quart.	*(It's quarter to five.)*
Il est cinq heures moins dix.	*(It's ten to five.)*
Il est cinq heures dix.	*(It's ten past five.)*

In a later scene you will be able to practise telling the time using the 24 hour clock.

65 **Essayons d'en trouver un.**
En is used here in conjunction with **un** to replace a noun previously mentioned. This construction is the equivalent of the English construction with *one*, in sentences such as: *I want one* **J'en veux un(e)**, *I have one* **J'en ai un(e)**, etc.

VOCABULARY

je vous en prie	don't mention it
passionnant	exciting
s'occuper (de)	to be in charge (of)
estimer beaucoup	to have a high opinion of
il faut que je voie	I must see
il vous plaira	you will like him
un genre	(a) kind
nous avons pris rendez-vous	we've fixed an appointment
en quoi que ce soit	in any way
manquer de faire quelque chose	to fail to do something
je n'y manquerai pas	I'll be sure to do so
rappeler	to remind

votre nom (*m.*)	your name
un visage	face
se rappeler	to remember
je me rappelle	I remember
puis-je	can I
quand-même	on the other hand, all the same
il faut que je rentre tout ça	I must move all this in

EXERCISE 5: Excuses and introductions

All the phrases in this exercise are very useful and commonly used in spoken French. Listen carefully and practise until you feel you know what to say in each of the situations illustrated.

LANGUAGE NOTES

1 **quelqu'un vient de s'excuser**
Venir de + a verb in the Infinitive; the phrase used to indicate that something has just happened.

8 **C'est moi qui m'excuse.**
Qui is a relative pronoun, meaning *who* or *which*. It introduces a new clause, and it is the subject of the verb placed directly after it.

31 **Je vous disais bien que je n'avais pas la mémoire des noms.**
In French the sequence of tenses is different from the English one: the second verb here is in the Imperfect tense, not in the Present tense as it would be in English: *I told you I CAN never remember names.*

VOCABULARY

s'excuser	to apologize
se présenter	to introduce oneself
ma faute	my fault
partout	everywhere
ça ne fait rien	it doesn't matter
navré(e)	very sorry

SCENE 6: Strasbourg – in the CGE offices

Catherine and Pierre are still trying to have a conversation
... They finally manage to find an empty office, and
Catherine proceeds to explain to Pierre what the Geneva
Project is all about. They are once again rudely
interrupted, and are asked to leave by the secretary who
wants to lock up before going home. Catherine, however,
succeeds in telling Pierre he is going to work in Geneva,
and that he is, in fact, due to start his new job next week.
Pierre is somewhat surprised, as he can't remember
signing anything to agree to such an arrangement ...

LANGUAGE NOTES

**Au bureau ... de Genève/Au siège du holding à Genève/
je pars pour Genève**
Make a note of the prepositions **à, de** and **pour**
used to indicate a location or destination.

17 **notre agence**
This is the possessive adjective corresponding to **nous,**
used to accompany a noun in the singular: *our agency.* All
the possessive adjectives are listed in the Appendix.

22 **vous, vous nous appartenez à nous**
Note the way to insist on the pronouns here, by using a
second pronoun emphasizing the first one. **Vous** stresses
the first **vous,** subject of the verb. **A nous** stresses the
indirect pronoun **nous.**

39 **Nous cherchions un bureau vide.**
Here the Imperfect tense is the equivalent of *We
were looking for an empty office.*

**ça n'a pas d'importance/Ça m'intéressait comme ça, en
passant./Ça vous concerne aussi.**
Ça is used all the time in French to refer to a general set of
events, to a given situation previously mentioned, and
also in many set phrases.

75 **je me rappelle y avoir pensé**   *I remember having thought of it*
Note that in French the Past Infinitive (**avoir** + Past Participle) is used.

77 **Il y a plusieurs mois.**
Here **Il y a** + expression of time (**mois, jours, années, heures, minutes**) is the equivalent of the English word *ago: several months ago.*

Pour que j'aille à Genève?/elle veut que nous partions
Note the Subjunctive in these two examples, after **pour que** and **vouloir que.**

87 **Quoi?**
This is a familiar way of registering surprise, incredulity even, at something someone has just said.

94 **Ça ne vous dérangerait pas d'aller ailleurs?**
The Conditional is used to make a polite suggestion; here, the secretary is signifying to Pierre and Catherine that she wants them to go somewhere else.

VOCABULARY

il doit y en avoir un	there must be one
ça a l'air d'aller	that seems to be OK
un siège	head office
une société mère	parent company
un holding	holding company
partir	to leave
non plus	not ... either
reprendre	to go over again
reprenons (tout)	let's go over (everything) again
depuis	from, since
le début	beginning
jusqu'ici	up to now
ça ne vous dérangerait pas	would you mind
(lui) arriver	to happen (to him)
un moyen	way, means
un seul moyen	only one way

EXERCISE 6: Describing a company. The days of the week.

Concentrate on trying to remember the vocabulary, and note also the phrases used to express dates and times: **samedi, la semaine prochaine, etc.**

LANGUAGE NOTES

13 **en Suisse, au Canada, en Grande-Bretagne**
En is used with names of countries which are feminine: **la France** so **en France, la Grande-Bretagne** so **en Grande-Bretagne,** etc. **Au** is used with names of countries which are masculine: **le Canada** so **au Canada.**

26 **un voyage à Genève**
A is used before names of towns to mean *in* or *to:* **à Genève** means either *in Geneva* or *to Geneva.*
Here it means *to Geneva.*

37 **ils pourront**
This is an example of a very irregular Future tense. Like the other verb forms you will find it listed in the Appendix at the back of the book.

VOCABULARY

une maison mère	parent company
une filiale	subsidiary
un, une propriétaire	owner
détenir	to control
elle détient	it controls
disponible	free, available
un endroit	place

Cassette 1   Side 2
You're going to Geneva

SCENE 1: Strasbourg – in the car and in Pierre's flat

Catherine and Pierre are in Pierre's apartment. They are
discussing the arrangements regarding Pierre's departure
and his arrival in Geneva. In Catherine's presence Pierre
listens to the messages recorded on his answering machine.
We hear a message left by Pascale, his secretary, briefing
him on what he already knows, in terms which are very
energetic, to say the least. It transpires that she agreed to
Pierre's things being moved out of his office, as he was
due to leave anyway ... She informs Pierre that she will
come and join him in Geneva on her return from holiday.
Pierre seems less than enthusiastic at the prospect. He
invites Catherine, much amused by it all, to dinner, but
she declines; she has too much to do.

LANGUAGE NOTES

22 **chez moi**
    Chez is the word used with someone's name to refer to
    their house or shop. For example:

        Chez elle   *at/to her house*
        Chez Pierre   *at/to Pierre's house*
        Chez le boucher   *at/to the butcher shop*

23 **Où étiez-vous ...? J'ai téléphoné trois fois**
    Note the difference in use between the Imperfect and the
    Perfect tense. The Imperfect depicts an action which lasts
    in the past; the Perfect tense is used to describe a series of
    actions which do not last.

51 **Il faudra que vous trouviez**
    You will remember that **il faut que** (here in the Future
    tense) is followed by the Subjunctive.

    ne descendez pas/Ne vous inquiétez pas
    Note the word order for the negative Imperative here.

VOCABULARY

une pièce	room
tarder	to delay
je ne vais pas tarder à partir	I won't be long before I leave
soit … soit	either … or
précipité	fast, rushed
vérifier	to check
un répondeur téléphonique	answering machine
des nouvelles (*f.***)**	some news
de votre part	on your behalf
ne vous inquiétez pas	don't worry
rejoindre	to join
penser à	to think of
elle pense vraiment à tout	she really thinks of everything
c'était d'accord	it was OK
plus rien	nothing else
vous allez me manquer	I'm going to miss you
envoyer	to send
j'enverrai	I'll send
s'en aller	to leave, go away
je vais m'en aller	I'm going to leave

EXERCISE 1: Listening to a message

A listening and comprehension exercise. Listen very carefully before answering the questions during the pauses.

LANGUAGE NOTES

je ne pourrai pas/Est-ce qu'elle partira …?/Je serai là
All these verbs are in the Future tense. It is a good idea to regularly check the verb tenses in the Appendix at the back of the book.

est-ce que je peux partir …?/Où est-ce qu'elle veut aller?
The verbs **pouvoir** and **vouloir** are followed by a verb in the Infinitive. There is no need for a preposition between the two.

VOCABULARY

le truc	thing, gadget
en panne	broken down
récupérer	to get back
devenir	to become, get
tout ça deviendra	all that will get

SCENE 2: Strasbourg – in the CGE offices

In this scene Pierre is talking to his office supervisor. He breaks the news that he is leaving for Geneva ... which Bernard, the supervisor, apparently knew anyway. Bernard gets increasingly irritated by Pierre's rather casual attitude regarding his sudden departure and the problems this is going to create for everyone in the department. It is the last straw when Pierre asks about his precious coffee machine: Bernard gives him a stern lecture and Pierre beats a quick but nevertheless philosophical retreat.

LANGUAGE NOTES

Henri va se retrouver seul/Je suis sûr qu'il s'en sortira
These are two very common phrases in French: **se retrouver,** meaning *to find oneself, to end up,* and **s'en sortir,** which means *to manage, to work it out, to pull through.*

40 **Elle est à moi**
This is another way of expressing possession in French: using the verb **être** + **à** + a pronoun (**moi, vous, lui,elle,** etc.). Compare the following:
   C'est ma cafetière.
   Elle est à moi.
   C'est la mienne.

44 **Je l'ai achetée le mois dernier**
The definite article **le/la/les** + the adjective **dernière** are used in French to say *last month, last week, last year,* etc.:
   Je suis allée en France *la semaine dernière*   (last week)
                              l'année dernière   (last year)

49 **Vous nous quittez dans quatre jours**
Note the use of **dans** to indicate that something is going to take place "IN four days' time". Similarly, you would say: **Je vais à Londres dans une semaine, Je pars pour Paris dans un mois,** etc.

52 **De gros problèmes**
   De is used instead of **des** before a group of words made up
   of an adjective + a noun in the plural.

   VOCABULARY

s'en sortir	to manage, come through
il s'en sortira	he'll manage, come through it OK
un embarras	difficult situation

EXERCISE 2: Dates and times

Listen, then practise answering during the pauses
provided.

LANGUAGE NOTES

11 **Ça fait six jours**
   This is the phrase used when reckoning a total (of days,
   months, money, etc.).
   Make a note of all these useful expressions of time and the
   tenses they are used with:

Aujourd'hui	**La semaine dernière**
Hier	**La semaine prochaine**
Demain	

41 **Catherine devait prendre l'avion ... aujourd'hui**
   Devoir is used here in the Imperfect in the sense of
   to be due to, to be supposed to.

   VOCABULARY

par conséquent	therefore
un délai trop court	too short notice
signifier	to mean
ce qui signifie	which means

SCENE 3: Geneva – at the airport and in Carole Heywood's car

Catherine is at Geneva airport. She is met by a woman called Carole Heywood, who is herself Swiss but is married to an Englishman living in Switzerland. She has come in her car to pick Catherine up and during the ride she talks a little about herself and her husband, who is looking for work at the moment. She gives Catherine the name of her hotel and tells her where it is situated. When they get to the hotel downtown, Carole expresses surprise at Catherine having so little luggage.

LANGUAGE NOTES

11 **D'où êtes-vous, vous-même?**
The preposition **de** is used to denote the origin of someone or something.

12 **Vous-même**
Is used to emphasize the subject, **vous.**

Je suis suisse/Je suis mariée à un Anglais
Adjectives of nationality do not take a capital letter, but nouns do.
   Je suis français.
   C'est un Français.

24 **Qu'est-ce qu'il fait, comme métier?**
Comme here means *as, in the way of: as a job.*

Facile de …/Utile de …
These two adjectives are followed by the verb in the Infinitive: **Facile d'être, utile de parler.**

VOCABULARY

vous-même	yourself
vivre	to live
vous vivez	you live
pas grand'chose	not much
enseigner	to teach
un étranger	a foreigner
un emploi	job
dur	hard, difficult
surtout	especially
se débrouiller	to get by, manage
je ne me débrouille pas trop mal	I get by quite well
bruyant	noisy
quoi que ce soit	anything at all, whatsoever
manquer	to fail
je n'y manquerai pas	I won't fail to do so, I'll make sure I do
compliqué	complicated, difficult
recevoir	to receive
je recevrai	I'll receive

EXERCISE 3: Jobs and nationalities

Pay particular attention, when doing this exercise, to the names of countries and the corresponding adjectives of nationality.

LANGUAGE NOTES

Il vient *de France*/Elle vient *d'Allemagne*
De/D' + feminine name of country

16 **Il vient *du Japon***
Du/D' + masculine name of country

31 **Comme professeur**
Another use of **comme** *as, in the way of.*

38 **Elle est employée de bureau**
No article with names of occupations in this sort of statement.

VOCABULARY

servir (à)	to be used (for, to)
qui servent à	which are used to
décrire	to describe
un homme d'affaires	businessman
au chômage	unemployed
lentement	slowly
une employée de bureau	office worker (woman)
un mari	husband

SCENE 4: Geneva – the offices of the Holding Company

In this scene we make the acquaintance of Alain Tanner, who works in the office building of the holding company. It is obvious that he and Catherine know each other very well, and even that they have in the past had some very pleasant times in Paris together. She asks him what it is like trying to find office space in Geneva. Alain Tanner explains there is no space available in the building, but that he has arranged for Catherine to see a real-estate agent immediately. In fact the appointment turns out to be for nine-thirty, that is to say right now. But before Catherine leaves, Alain manages to invite her to dinner. It seems he has not changed ...

LANGUAGE NOTES

10 **Et l'hôtel, il vous convient?**
Note the emphatic turn of phrase: the pronoun **il** refers back to the noun, **hôtel**.

32 *Il est peut-être préférable que* **nous ne** *soyons* **pas dans ce bâtiment**
Le mieux, c'est que **vous lui** *parliez* **directement**
Two examples of the Subjunctive being used with a set expression.

VOCABULARY

convenir (à)	to suit
il vous convient?	is it to your satisfaction?
de bons moments	nice times
en avance	ahead
tellement	so
de toute façon	in any case, anyway
que nous ne soyons pas	that we shouldn't be
un agent immobilier	realtor
rencontrer	to meet
pour que vous le rencontriez	for you to meet him
rien ne presse	there's no rush
à quel sujet?	about what?

EXERCISE 4: Telling the time

You have already learnt, or been reminded of, how to tell the time in French. In this practice, the 24 hour clock is used, so you know how to use both systems. The 24 hour clock is mostly used for timetables, official appointments, train and plane departure and arrival times.

LANGUAGE NOTES

11 **Dix-sept heures quarante/dix-neuf heures quinze etc.**
Here are, illustrated below, a few examples of the two systems for telling the time.

Quelle heure est-il?

Il est quatre heures moins vingt-cinq de l'après-midi.	*(3.35 pm)*	**Il est quinze heures trente-cinq.**
Il est neuf heures et demie du soir.	*(9.30 pm)*	**Il est vingt-et-une heures trente.**
Il est onze heures moins le quart du soir.	*(10.45 pm)*	**Il est vingt-deux heures quarante-cinq.**
Il est trois heures moins dix de l'après-midi.	*(2.50 pm)*	**Il est quatorze heures cinquante.**

46 **Le voilà**
Le/la/les voilà: note this way of saying *he/she/they is/are.*

VOCABULARY

l'heure *(f.)*	time
lire l'heure	to tell the time
environ	about
une horaire	timetable
utiliser	to use
l'horloge	clock
on utilise l'horloge de vingt-quatre heures	the 24-hour clock is used
vouloir dire	to mean
qu'est-ce que ça veut dire?	what does that mean?
au lieu de	instead of
un peu mieux	a little better
une agence de voyage	a travel agent

SCENE 5: Strasbourg – at a travel agency

Pierre is at a travel agent's. He is booking his flight to
Geneva. There is no direct flight there; one has to catch a
connection in Paris. The clerk suggests that Pierre should
take the plane and the TGV instead of catching two planes
but Pierre decides he prefers the latter. The clerk then
issues him a one-way ticket to Geneva, which Pierre
pays for by cheque.

LANGUAGE NOTES

7 **N'importe laquelle**
Laquelle is the feminine singular form of the word
meaning *any (one)*. It refers to **compagnie**.

VOCABULARY

une agence de voyage	travel agency
ça m'est égal	I don't mind
n'importe laquelle	any one (company)
disons	let's say
apparemment	apparently
un vol	flight
ensuite	then, next
durer	to last
un voyage	journey
il dure	it lasts
une correspondance	connection
le TGV (train à grande vitesse)	high-speed train
aller	to go
il faudra que j'aille de l'aéroport jusqu'à la gare	I will have to go from the airport to the station
un aller et retour	round-trip ticket
un aller simple	one-way ticket
une attente	(a) wait
régler	to pay
une carte de crédit	a credit card
en liquide	cash
à quel ordre?	to whom?
établir (un chèque)	to write (a check)

EXERCISE 5: Buying a ticket

Listen carefully making sure you understand everything, then do the exercise, answering during the pauses. Make a note, as you go along, of the vocabulary, the polite requests, the way of saying a date.

LANGUAGE NOTES

En avion/à Paris/pour Paris
Note the use of **en** to indicate the means of transport and of **à, pour** to indicate the destination.

Pouvez-vous me réserver une place?/Quand voulez-vous revenir?
The word order (verb first) makes these questions very formal. This is the tone usually adopted in a formal, conventional situation such as this one.

23 **Le vendredi 4 juin**
Note the way of giving the date in French, which is quite different from the English way.

46 **Il est en train de se faire un ami**
This phrase is used all the time in French, to express the fact that someone is in the process of doing something. (Also note in passing the way of saying *to make friends with somebody* in French: **se faire un ami**.)

VOCABULARY

faire	to make
ça faisait	that made
pas mal de	quite a few
ouvert	open
se faire un ami	to make friends

SCENE 6: Strasbourg – the airport departure lounge: on board the plane

We are following Pierre as he boards the plane at Strasbourg airport, and then during the flight to Geneva. At the airport, he makes the acquaintance of a Mr. Melville, who says he is a business consultant. He listens to Pierre talk about his job in detail, and gives him his card, saying that, thanks to his many contacts in government circles, he could probably send some work his way. He finally suggests that Pierre send him a detailed plan for an engineering project. Pierre is delighted and agrees enthusiastically.

LANGUAGE NOTES

10 **Vous y allez seulement en touriste**
Another use of **en**; here, it means *as: as a tourist.*

26 *Imaginez que vous ayez* **une ville d'un million d'habitants**
The Subjunctive is used here to refer to something which is not a fact, but a supposition. The same applies to the sentence **Il se peut que je puisse,** a bit further on in the text.

42 **Nous faisons exécuter le projet intégral par les entreprises de notre groupe.**
Faire + Infinitive + **par** + noun.
This construction is used all the time in French. It means *to have something done by someone/something.*

75 **La façon dont nous travaillerions**
Make a note of this turn of phrase **La façon dont** (one also says **la manière dont ...**): *the way, the manner in which ...*

79 **Veuillez éteindre vos cigarettes**
This way of asking someone to do something is very formal and only used in this type of situation. It is the sort of request which one can see written in trains or buses, for instance.

VOCABULARY

une salle d'embarquement	departure lounge
à bord de	on board
munis de	holding
marron	brown
une carte d'embarquement	boarding card
priés (de)	requested, asked (to)
en touriste	as a tourist
une formation	training
un moyen	(a) means
un transport en commun	public transport
souterrain	underground
exposer	to explain
nous vous exposons	we explain to you
soumettre	to present
mettre au point (un projet)	to draw up (a plan)
fournir	to provide
exécuter	to carry out
nous faisons exécuter le projet	we have the project carried out
un matériel	equipment
une locomotive	locomotive, engine
compétitif	competitive
que	whom, which
il se peut que	it's possible that
pouvoir	to be able to
diriger sur	to put someone on the track of
une affaire	business deal
conseiller	to advise
une entreprise	firm, business
des milieux	circles
faire appel à vous	to ask for your help
citer	to quote
Moyen-Orient	Middle East
un délai	deadline
atterrir	to land
éteindre	to put out
une ceinture (de sécurité)	safety-belt
débuter	to start
prochain(e)	next

Cassette 2   Side 1

What are the new offices like?

SCENE 1: Geneva – an empty office

In this scene, a real-estate agent is showing Catherine around an empty office. According to what he tells her on the way there, it is very well situated, in one of the most elegant districts in Geneva. Catherine looks at everything in detail and plans to change a few things: make the reception area smaller, the office area itself bigger. The realtor confirms that this should be no problem. After checking on a few details with the agent, (rent: three months in advance; lease: three years, with the possibility of renewing it), Catherine goes back to the realtor's office to deal with formalities.

LANGUAGE NOTES

10 **C'est au troisième étage**
Au is the preposition used to indicate the floor.

32 **Elle fait combien?**
This way of asking a question, by keeping the same word order as for a statement and putting the interrogative word at the end, is very common in French conversation. (Cf. **C'est grand comment?**)

33 **Environ six mètres sur cinq**
Note the use of **sur** when giving measurements.
Environ can be placed before or after the word it modifies.

51 **Cette partie-ci**   *This part*
The demonstrative adjective is in two parts in French. In fact **-ci** is only used if one wants to contrast something or someone (placed near the person speaking) to something or someone else placed further away.

50 **Celui-là**
This is the demonstrative pronoun, for the masculine singular, meaning *that one*.

VOCABULARY

un quartier	area, neighborhood
pratique	convenient
un immeuble	building
un étage	floor
un ascenseur	elevator
un escalier	stairs
un mètre carré	square metre
suffire	to be enough
auparavant	before
des locataires (*m.f.*)	tenants
des toilettes (*f.*)	toilets
un distributeur de boissons	vending machine
elle fait combien?	how large is it?
six mètres sur cinq	six meters by five
où donne le soleil?	where does the sunlight come from?
clair	light, sunny
le sud	the south
une prise de téléphone	telephone jack
une prise de courant	electrical outlet
abattre	to knock down
agrandir	to extend
rétrécir	to reduce (the size of)
remplir (des formalités)	to carry out, complete (formalities)
enlever	to remove
ajouter	to add
un loyer	rent
d'avance	in advance
un bail	lease
renouveler	to renew
régler	to complete, settle

EXERCISE 1: Description of an office

There are many idiomatic phrases to remember in this exercise, especially the ones which are used to give measurements and to describe an office. Listen to the dialogues, try and reply in the pauses provided.

LANGUAGE NOTES

C'est un immeuble moderne/Il est au troisième étage
You have come across **c'est** very often already, used in different ways. It is sometimes difficult for students to decide when to use **c'est,** and when to use **il/elle est** when referring to an object, or to an event. There are as always exceptions, but in general one can say that **C'est + un/une/ des** is used when the thing in question has not yet been mentioned whereas **il/elle est** is used to refer to something which has been previously mentioned. In the above examples, **il** refers to **le bureau.**

36 **Tous les trois mois**
Tous les (feminine **toutes**) is used to indicate that that something is happening at regular intervals: **tous les jours, toutes les semaines, tous les ans,** etc.

37 **Par trimestre**
Par is used to indicate how often something occurs in a given time span, and is used in numerous phrases, such as: **par jour, par mois, par an,** etc.

VOCABULARY

un terme	term, word
technique	technical
concernant	regarding, to do with
décrire	to describe
se composer de	to be made up of
une réunion	mceting
une salle de conférence	conference room
soit	that is
chacun	each (one)
un endroit	place
se trouver	to be located
se trouve	is located
un total de	a total of
en tout	in all, altogetlier
des arrêts d'autobus	bus stops
un bâtiment	building
au rez-de-chaussée	on the ground floor
la boutique	shop
se monter à	to come to
se monte à	comes to
par an	per year
un trimestre	quarter (three months)
tous les trois mois	every three months (every quarter)
au bout de	at the end of
se retrouver	to meet up again
ils se sont retrouvés	they have met up again

SCENE 2: The Geneva office

Pierre finally manages to locate Catherine after taking the wrong turn on the third floor and getting lost for a while. Catherine shows him round their new offices and Pierre is favourably impressed. He makes sure the phones are working, and they discuss getting a receptionist-secretary. Pierre will give Alain Tanner a ring to get some help in finding a suitable candidate. At the end of the scene we learn that Pierre is about to set off on his travels once again ...

LANGUAGE NOTES

5 **Je vous ai cherchée partout**
The **e** at the end of **cherchée** refers to **vous** (= Catherine). When the direct object complement of a verb is, as here, a pronoun, and is placed before the verb conjugated with **avoir,** then the Past Participle (here, **cherchée**) agrees with the complement. Here, it is in the feminine singular, as **vous** refers to a noun which is feminine singular (Catherine).

VOCABULARY

partout	everywhere
assez de	enough (+ *noun*)
un espace	space
branché	connected, plugged
faux	wrong
un numéro	number
un télex	telex machine
une photocopieuse	photocopier
mal	bad
un chef	boss, chief
c'est vous le chef	you're the boss
taper à la machine	to type
un coup de fil	phone call
un ordinateur	computer
entendu	agreed
fonctionner	to work

EXERCISE 2: Office equipment

This is a fairly straightforward exercise, so you can, if you want, concentrate on the pronunciation and fluency of your responses as well as on their content.

LANGUAGE NOTES

1 **J'aimerais vérifier**
Polite request, expressed through the use of the Conditional **J'aimerais.**

14 **Qu'est-ce que c'est que ça?**
The addition of **ça** after **qu'est-ce que c'est?** emphasizes the surprise in the question. The implication is that the person asking the question has absolutely no idea what the thing is.

VOCABULARY

ranger	to keep
un classeur	file
un fichier	file cabinet
la machine à écrire	typewriter
un engin	machine, gadget
un chiffre	figure
une calculatrice	calculator
de l'aide (*f.*)	(some) help

SCENE 3: Geneva – the offices of the Holding Company

Pierre goes to see Alain Tanner. He asks him for help in finding a receptionist-secretary and a flat for himself. Tanner suggests different ways of dealing with the first query. As for Pierre's flat, it seems that everything has already been taken care of by some mysterious person.

LANGUAGE NOTES

26 **Le plus tôt sera le mieux**
Note the superlative form here: **le plus** + adjective.

44 **La fille ... dit qu'elle est sûre qu'il y a un logement ...**
Whereas in English *that* is constantly dropped between two sentences, in French **que** must be included in spoken as well as in written French. **La fille dit qu'elle est sûre** *the girl says she's sure*.

47 **C'est quelqu'un de Strasbourg qui a tout arrangé**
Another way of stressing a part of a sentence, using the construction with **C'est ... qui ...**

54 **Quelle peste!**
You already know **quel/quelle** as interrogative words (**Quelle était la deuxième chose?**). They are also used in exclamatory sentences, and are the equivalent of the English *What! What a ...!*

VOCABULARY

il nous faut	we need
une annonce	ad, notice
bilingue	bilingual
trilingue	trilingual
un logement	accommodation
de fonction	which goes with the job
ça n'a pas d'importance	it doesn't matter
sans doute	probably
qualifiée	qualified
d'abord	first
consulter	to consult

un personnel	staff, employees
le service du personnel	Personnel department
bien entendu	of course
le plus tôt ...	the sooner ...
le mieux	the better
un associé	associate, colleague
sûr	sure
le même	the same
un étage	floor
au même étage	on the same floor
arranger	to arrange, to organize
d'accord	OK
il sera	he will be
de retour	back
se mettre à	to start (doing something)
à la recherche de	looking for

EXERCISE 3: Polite questions

This is a straightforward exercise which offers an ideal opportunity for you to practise your pronunciation and intonation.

LANGUAGE NOTES

Comment allez-vous?/Comment vont les affaires?/Tout va bien?
Note these useful expressions with the verb **aller.**

Trop de travail/Pas assez d'argent
Beaucoup de/Trop de/Assez de + noun in the singular or the plural: all expressions of quantity.

VOCABULARY

poli	polite
amical	friendly
occupé	busy
tirer l'histoire au clair	to sort out, clear up
arriver	to happen
ce qui lui arrive	what happens to him

SCENE 4: Geneva – the offices of the Holding Company

Where we learn more about Pierre's flat, or rather flats …
In this scene he is talking to Mr Chambon, the person
responsible for providing staff with accommodations.
Pierre's secretary, Pascale, has phoned from Strasbourg
and reserved two flats next to each other, one for her and
one for Pierre. The latter tries very hard to undo this
arrangement, and to convince Mr Chambon that what he
really wants is a very, very small flat on his own. Mr
Chambon promises he'll try to help …

LANGUAGE NOTES

55 **Plus il sera petit, mieux ce sera**
Note the word order with these comparatives: it remains
the same as in a normal sentence.
Comparative + subject + verb, comparative + subject
+ verb.

57 **Quelque chose de vraiment petit**
You have already met **quelque chose d'autre** *something
else*. This is the same type of expression: **quelque chose de
petit** *something small*.
    Quelque chose + de + adjective.

VOCABULARY

en ce moment	at the moment
d'un instant à l'autre	any moment now
s'asseoir	to sit down
envoyer	to send
convenir (à quelqu'un)	to suit (someone)
dans l'immédiat	in the immediate future
là-bas	over there
un cadre	executive
un malentendu	misunderstanding
une demande	request
cher	expensive
bon marché	cheap
une garçonnière	bachelor apartment
un célibataire	bachelor
fou, folle	mad, crazy

EXERCISE 4: Correcting someone

This is a practice mainly about vocabulary. The language itself is quite simple, so you could take this opportunity to practise your pronunciation, if you feel like it.
inté*r*essé, e*rr*eur (**r** sound);
mal**heureu**sement, *deux* (**eu** sound),
eu (**Je crains qu'il n'y ait *eu***) (**u** sound);
manière (**ère** sound);
mal*enten*du (nasal sound **en** not sounded),
u sound needs some practising to get it right!

LANGUAGE NOTES

4 **Ce qui m'a intéressé, c'est ...**
Once again, the emphatic form is used, with **c'est.**

15 **Je crois que vous faites erreur**
After **je crois que** the word order is the same as in a simple sentence and there is no need to use the Subjunctive.

VOCABULARY

rectifications (*f.*)	corrections
faire	to do
avoir l'impression (que)	to have the feeling, to be under the impression, (that)
j'ai l'impression (que)	it seems to me (that)
la manière (dont)	the way (in which)
se tromper	to make a mistake, to get something wrong
une erreur	mistake
coûter	to cost
qui coûte cher	expensive

SCENE 5: The Geneva office

Catherine has gathered all the members of her team
around her in order to introduce them to each other.
While they are waiting for the last two people to arrive,
Catherine gives Pierre a letter. It comes from the dreadful
Pascale, who is holidaying on the Costa Brava and wishes
to inform Pierre of the arrangements she has made. Pierre
is less than pleased on reading all this. Catherine interrupts
his grumbling comments to introduce him to his two
colleagues who have just arrived.

LANGUAGE NOTES

7   **Je veux vous présenter les uns aux autres**
Note the way in which reciprocity is expressed here:
literally, the sentence means *I want to introduce you the
ones to the others.*

Trop de problèmes/Trop de travail
Trop de, like **beaucoup de,** can be followed by words in the
singular or in the plural.

33   **... pour qu'ils nous réservent deux appartements**
Pour que, like several other expressions, is followed by a
verb in the Subjunctive. You will find a list of all these
expressions in the Appendix at the back of this book.

43   **Rien d'important**
This is the same construction as in **quelque chose d'autre,
quelque chose de petit.**

69   **... bien qu'en fait il vienne du service juridique**
Another of those expressions mentioned above: **vienne** is
the Present Subjunctive of the verb **venir.**

VOCABULARY

une équipe	team
au complet	assembled, all here
gentil	nice, kind
sympathique	friendly, nice, pleasant
modeste	modest, self-effacing
quel culot!	what nerve!
un séjour	stay
se mêler de	to interfere
de quoi se mêle-t-elle	it's none of her business
apporter	to bring
elle vous apporte ...?	is it bringing you ...?
se charger de	to take care of
je me charge de tout	I'll take care of everything
dès que	as soon as
retourner (à)	to go back (to)
quelle peste!	what a nuisance!
l'ingénierie (f.)	engineering
réalisable	feasible
tenir	to hold
il tient	he holds
les cordons de la bourse	purse strings
la bourse	purse
être chargé de	to be responsible for
un siège social	head office
bien qu'il vienne	although he comes
la vente	sales
le droit	law
un service juridique	legal department
une réussite	success
souhaiter	to wish, hope
je le souhaite	I hope it will be (a success)

EXERCISE 5: Introductions

Another straightforward and easy exercise to help you use various forms of greeting correctly. When you are listening to the recording, you could pay particular attention to the intonation this time, and try to reproduce it when it is your turn to speak.

LANGUAGE NOTES

1 **Laissons-les faire connaissance**
Note the word order: **laisser** + pronoun + Infinitve of verb.

6 **Ce n'est pas quelqu'un de la société Amiéra?**
This type of question implies that one is in fact fairly sure who the person in question is. One would expect an affirmative answer here.

VOCABULARY

les présentations (*f.*)	introductions
faire connaissance	to get to know (each other)
approfondir	to investigate
le service du marketing	the marketing department
enchanté(e)/très heureux(se)	pleased to meet you
comptabilité	accounts

SCENE 6: The Geneva office

At the beginning of the scene, Pierre is talking to Olivier
Rossi, who is the firm's accountant. He would like some
help in drawing up a list of prices and costs for a sample
specification he has done. Olivier warns him that the
figures he will produce can only apply to the particular
project Pierre has studied, and can't be applied to any
other project for any other town, but Pierre already
knows that. He doesn't need all the details. We then hear
Pierre dictating two letters: one to Mr Melville, to tell him
he is sending the information Melville had asked for. The
other to Pascale – which Pierre will pretend is from the
administrative officer. In it he tells her that unfortunately
it is not possible to find two flats next to one another as
she had requested, and that the only thing they could find
for ... Mr Boyer was a very small, one-room flat. Having
done this, Pierre goes to see Catherine to tell her about his
encounter with Melville, and his initiative in sending him
information about the kind of work they do in the
company. He is obviously hopeful that Catherine will
approve, but her reaction is not quite what he expected ...

LANGUAGE NOTES

8 **Vous avez bien traité ...?**
   You will recognize this use of **bien** in a question, to elicit a
   positive answer.

20 **C'est plus un document de marketing qu'un document
    financier**
    You have met this form of comparison with **plus ... que**
    more than once now.

26 **Vous m'aviez demandé de vous fournir ...**
    Note the construction **de** + a verb in the Infinitive.
    You will find in the Appendix at the back of the book a list
    of the verbs which can be followed by a verb in the
    Infinitive, with the preposition (**à** or **de**) which
    accompanies them.

84 **Il m'a dit avoir de bons contacts ...**
Note this construction with **dire,** using only a verb in the
Infinitive. Another way of expressing this would be:
> **Il m'a dit** *qu'il avait de bons contacts ...*

The construction with the Infinitive is only possible if it is
the same person who is the subject of the two verbs.

Chez notre plus grand concurrent/Chez C.M.A.
More examples of the use of **chez.** It can mean *at/to*
someone's house, but also *at/to someone's firm,* as it does
here.

VOCABULARY

un comptable	accountant
les coûts	the costs
traiter	to organize a transaction
vous avez bien traité	you did organize a transaction
l'Arabie Saoudite	Saudi Arabia
étudier	to study
comprendre	to include
qui comprend	including
un descriptif	abstract
les services (*m.*)	the services
un habitant	inhabitant
forcément	necessarily
appliquer	to apply
plus ... que	more ... than
un document	document
financier	financial
approximatif	approximate
ci-joint	enclosed
point	period
ainsi que	as well as
veuillez	please
faire parvenir	to forward
un courrier	letter
le courrier	mail
un retard	delay
une installation	moving-in
mouvementé	hectic

mettre en place	to set up
dans l'attente de vous lire	looking forward to hearing from you
agréer	to accept
je vous prie d'agréer ...	yours faithfully
actuellement	at the moment
à la ligne	new paragraph
disponible	available
un studio	studio apartment
un directeur administratif	administrative director
à l'avenir	in future
par hasard	by chance
un niveau	level
sympathique	friendly, nice
étonner	to surprise
un directeur des ventes	sales manager
convaincre	to convince
convaincu	convinced

Cassette 2   Side 2
I'm going to Paris

SCENE 1: The Geneva office

Catherine and Pierre are having a talk about work. Pierre remarks that he has not seen Catherine for a long time. She says she has been very busy. He goes on to say that unfortunately he isn't. Catherine asks him what his timetable for the coming week is: he is going to Paris on the Wednesday for three days, and is going to interview an applicant today for the post of secretary. Nothing else for the rest of the week. Pierre finds this a little depressing. Catherine tries to comfort him by saying that the company is only starting and that they should get more busy very soon. In the meantime, she invites Pierre to come with her to have a look at the computer centre. But Pierre can't as Catherine is going there just at the time of his interview. We leave Pierre bored, wondering what he can do next.

LANGUAGE NOTES

4 **Ça fait longtemps que je ne vous ai pas vue**
Remember this way of saying that one has not done something for a long time. Another way of expressing the same idea would be to use **il y a: Il y a longtemps que je ne vous ai pas vue.**

17 **Je pars pour Paris mercredi**
As in English, the Present tense is used in French to refer to something which is going to take place in the future, usually the fairly near future.

Rien à faire/Trop à faire
There are several constructions with the Infinitive in this scene.

34 **Pour lancer ce genre de projet**
Another expression with the Infinitive, which you will remember means *in order to* ...

Je partirai d'ici vers onze heures et demie/Je vous verrai plus tard

Here the plain Future tense is used as an alternative way to indicate that the speaker is making a decision to do something in the (fairly near) future.

VOCABULARY

pris	busy
lire	to read
je lis	I'm reading
justement	precisely
prévoir	to plan
votre programme	your schedule
vous avez prévu?	have you planned?
sinon	otherwise
la commission de liaison	liaison committee
le poste	job
une entrevue	interview
déprimant	depressing
lancer	to launch
ce genre de (projet)	this kind of (project)
avoir	to have
vous aurez	you will have
ce n'est pas drôle	it's not much fun
un centre informatique	computer centre
vers	at about, roughly

EXERCISE 1: Plans

As well as concentrating on the vocabulary in this exercise, you can give your attention to the tenses and the change in the tenses used: Present, Perfect, Future tense. Also note the different ways of expressing the Future tense you will hear at the end of the exercise.

LANGUAGE NOTES

2 **J'aimerais bien réentendre ...**
J'aimerais corresponds to the English *I would like.* It is the formula used to introduce a polite request.

On dirait qu'il y a .../On dirait que toutes ces constructions signifient
The Conditional is used here again in this set phrase: **On dirait que,** which corresponds to the English expression: *It looks as if ..., It would seem that.*

45 **Quoi qu'il en soit ...**
Note the use of the Subjunctive in this set phrase.

VOCABULARY

un emploi du temps	timetable
un planning	schedule, program
un rapport	report
être de retour	to be back
je serai de retour	I'll be back
exprimer	to express
une tournure	turn of phrase
déjeuner	to have lunch
vers	about
quoi qu'il en soit	be that as it may
un candidat (une candidate)	applicant

SCENE 2: The Geneva office

Pierre is interviewing Françoise for the post of secretary. He starts by offering her some coffee, and then proceeds to ask her some questions. First, what she is doing at the moment: in what way she uses her languages, what her speed is in shorthand and typing, whether she likes typing. He ends the interview by asking her if she thinks she would mind working on her own, and why she wishes to leave her present job. Pierre thanks her and tells her that they will let her know their answer by the end of the week.

LANGUAGE NOTES

8 **C'est moi, Pierre Boyer**
   Again, we have an example here of how to emphasize a word in French, using **c'est.**

13 **La voilà**
   Remember this way of saying *there it is* (for the feminine singular) in French. **Le voilà** is the masculine singular form. **Les voilà** is the form for the plural.

14 **Avant que nous ne commencions**
   Some expressions, such as **de peur que, de crainte que,** are followed by **ne** and by the Subjunctive. Ne is placed directly before the verb. This is a fairly formal construction, not used very often in everyday, informal spoken French.

19 **J'avais une très bonne cafetière électrique**
   The Imperfect tense refers here to a state of affairs which existed in the past. Pierre *used to* own a coffee machine.

VOCABULARY

un entretien	interview
en avance	early
volontiers	willingly, I'd love one
actuellement	at present
une maison	company
utiliser	to use
utile	useful
une langue	language
un niveau	level
la dactylo(graphie)	typing
la sténo(graphie)	shorthand
une vitesse de frappe	typing speed
un entraînement (*m.*)	practice
une dactylo(graphe)	typist
la plupart (de)	most (of)
pas grand'chose	not much
attirer	to attract
sa propre secrétaire	his own secretary
muter	to transfer
tenir (quelqu'un) au courant	to keep (somebody) informed
nous vous tiendrons au courant	we will keep you informed
prendre une décision	to make a decision
contacter	to get in touch with

EXERCISE 2: Interviews

This is obviously a very useful exercise, as it enables you
to go over various questions which are frequently
asked in all kinds of different situations in everyday life.
It also shows clearly how to switch from indirect questions
(**Demandez-lui quelles sont ses qualifications**) to direct
questions (**Quelles sont vos qualifications?**).

LANGUAGE NOTES

3   ... **que l'on pose**
L'on is used instead of plain **on** when **on** is preceded by a
vowel, to facilitate pronunciation and because it sounds
better in more formal speech.

9   **Quel âge avez-vous?/J'ai trente ans**
Remember that in French the verb used to give someone's
age is **avoir.**

VOCABULARY

sembler	to seem
des études (*f.*)	studies
un certificat d'études commerciales	diploma in business studies
étudier	to study
un institut de technologie	technical school
une expérience	experience
le commerce	commerce, business
actuellement	at the moment
précédent	previous
les assurances	insurance
un employé de bureau	office worker
rester	to stay
y êtes-vous resté?	did you stay (there)?
une langue étrangère	foreign language
apprendre	to learn
j'ai appris	I learned
tenir (quelqu'un) au courant	to keep (someone) informed
l'heure du déjeuner	lunchtime

55

SCENE 3: Geneva – a café

In this scene we are in the company of Pierre and
Catherine who are having lunch together in a café. Pierre
thinks Catherine seems very young to be holding such a
responsible position in the company, and he asks her some
rather indiscreet questions: how old she is, and whether
she ever felt like getting married. Catherine answers them
quite candidly, and then she asks Pierre about his
interview with Françoise. Pierre thinks she is exactly the
person they are looking for; Catherine just wants to
make sure she can start as soon as possible, as they need
someone straight away.

LANGUAGE NOTES

20 **Comme je vous disais ...**
Comme has here the meaning of *as, like: As I was telling
you.*

25 **Vous n'êtes pas une femme**
We saw earlier on in the course that **un, une** and **des**
become **de** after a negative word like **pas** or **jamais.**
However, here, the meaning is *not a.* It is not *no*
or *not any.*

VOCABULARY

un endroit	place
cher	expensive
celui-là, celle-là	that one *(m.f.)*
vexer	to annoy
je ne vous vexe pas	I'm not annoying you
exercer (une profession)	to exercise, practise (a profession)
une position	position, post
tout à fait	quite (completely)
peut-être	perhaps
de toute façon	anyway, in any case
avoir de la chance	to be lucky
j'ai eu de la chance	I've been lucky
avoir envie de	to want to, to feel like
vous n'avez jamais eu envie	you've never wanted, felt like
se marier	to get married
pendant	for
marcher	to work, work out
ça n'a pas marché	it didn't work out
peu importe	it doesn't matter
au fait	by the way
ça s'annonce bien	it augurs well, it's a good start
faire l'affaire	to be suitable
elle fera l'affaire	she'll be suitable, she'll do
sympathique	pleasant
une connaissance (de)	a knowledge (of)
faire confiance (à quelqu'un)	to trust (somebody)
je vous fais confiance	I trust you (your judgment)
en ce qui me concerne	as far as I'm concerned
contacter	to get in touch (with)

EXERCISE 3: Listening and understanding (1)

This is a straightforward comprehension exercise. You don't have to tackle the whole conversation at once if it proves too much for you. Work your way through a few sentences at a time if you find this easier.

LANGUAGE NOTES

3 **Tu dois y avoir déjà goûté**
   Y is used as a pronoun with some verbs which take the preposition **à.** The verb here is **goûter à (un cocktail vodka/jus d'orange).** **Y** replaces the group of words **à un cocktail vodka – jus d'orange avec sucre.** In the same way, with the verb **penser (à quelque chose),** y is the pronoun used to replace **à** + a group of words. For example:
   Tu penses souvent à ton pays? Oui, j'y pense souvent.

34 **Qu'est-ce qu'il y a dedans?**
   Dedans means *in it* (understood here: *in the cocktail*).

56 **Cet après-midi**
   Cet is used instead of **ce** for the masculine when the next word starts with a vowel, for euphonic reasons.

VOCABULARY

goûter (à quelque chose)	to taste (something)
tu dois y avoir déjà goûté	you must have already tasted it
à la mode de	in the style of
habillé	dressed
une boisson	a drink
fort	strong
encore une fois	once again
évidemment	obviously
tout le monde	everybody
le thème	theme

SCENE 4: The Geneva office

Pierre is with Catherine. He confirms that Françoise can start on Monday. Then Catherine shows him an invitation to a conference which is due to take place in Paris on Thursday. As Pierre will already be in Paris, he decides he will go to the conference. Catherine will let the organisers know that he will attend, and she will ask someone called Gérard Floret to meet Pierre there. We leave Pierre booking a flight to Paris and a hotel room on the phone.

LANGUAGE NOTES

Lundi/jeudi/mercredi
The name of the day without any article can mean, as here: *this coming* or *next Monday, Thursday, Wednesday.* It can also mean *last Monday, Thursday, Wednesday.* You will also note that names of the days of the week do not take a capital letter in French, except of course after a period.

Ça a l'air un peu technique/Ça a l'air très intéressant
Avoir l'air is the French equivalent of the English verbs *to look/to seem.* Also note the use of **ça** in all these expressions.

VOCABULARY

bien entendu	naturally, obviously, of course
le système de contrôle intégré	integrated control system
plutôt	rather
dans vos cordes	up your alley
mesquin	stingy, petty
prévenir	to warn, to let (someone) know
à partir de	from
manquer	to miss
il ne manque jamais	he never misses
d'autre part	in addition

EXERCISE 4: Spelling (2)

You will have to spell words out in many different situations, for instance on the phone. So here is a chance to practise spelling. As well as checking your answers against the recording, you could also check your pronunciation of the letters, especially those which contain a sound which does not exist in English ... such as **o, u, é** and **r.** Concentrate in particular on the vowel sounds, which are short and clear-cut in French.

LANGUAGE NOTES

J'ai appris à épeler/... j'aimerais bien m'exercer à épeler
Two verbs: **apprendre** and **s'exercer à,** which take the preposition **à** and the Infinitive. Remember that you will find a list of the verbs taking **à** or **de** + the Infinitive in the Appendix.

19 **Genève**
This word is spelled in the recording, and you will notice the mention made of the grave accent on the second **e:e accent grave.** There are, of course, two other kinds of accent.
accent aigu   é spelled **e accent aigu**
and
accent circonflexe ê spelled **e accent circonflexe**

VOCABULARY

épeler	to spell
tout haut	aloud
majuscule	capital (letter)
un trait d'union	hyphen
juste	correct

SCENE 5: Paris – Pierre's hotel

In this scene Pierre is having a few problems with the hotel night porter, who is less than cooperative in tracing his reservation and making him welcome. Finally, after filling in a form and grudgingly agreeing to pay in advance, Pierre manages to get a room to sleep in.

LANGUAGE NOTES

1 **Alors ça vient?**
This expression indicates impatience and is not to be used unless one wishes to be deliberately rude!

11 **Une chambre à un lit/à deux lits**
A here has the meaning of **avec**.

35 **Un responsable**
Note how the adjective is used as a noun here.

Mais enfin, qu'est-ce que ça veut dire?/C'est un hôtel ici, oui ou non?
These two sentences again betray Pierre's impatience. **Mais enfin** and **oui ou non?** should not be used unless one wishes to show that one is getting angry! Also, **qu'est-ce que ça veut dire?** is not merely an enquiry, but also an an expression of impatience.

VOCABULARY

une chambre à un lit/à deux lits	a single/double room
une douche	shower
remplir	to fill in
remplissez ça	fill that in
avoir du retard	to be late
mon avion a eu du retard	my plane was late, delayed
par écrit	in writing
d'avance	in advance
un secrétariat	(secretary's) office
responsable	responsible, in charge
un responsable	someone in charge
de service	on duty

EXERCISE 5: Booking a hotel room

You have already done a practice of this kind, in which you had to put into direct speech a question which was formulated indirectly. It also gives you the opportunity to practise prices and numbers and their pronunciation.

LANGUAGE NOTES

Here is a quick summary of a few direct questions and how they can be translated into indirect speech:

Direct speech	Indirect speech
Combien de temps est-ce qu'il veut rester?	
Combien de temps veut-il rester?	**Le client va dire combien de temps il veut rester.**
Il veut rester combien de temps?	
Est-ce qu'il veut une chambre à un lit?	**Il doit dire s'il veut une chambre à un lit.**
Qu'est-ce qui est compris dans ces cent quatre-vingt-dix francs?	**Il veut savoir ce qui est compris dans ces cent quatre-vingt-dix francs.**
C'est cent quatre-vingt-dix francs.	**Disons que c'est cent quatre-vingt-dix francs.**

VOCABULARY

à la fois	at one time
compris	included
comprendre	to include
ça comprend ...?	does that include ...?
une clef	key
se lever	to get up
réveiller (quelqu'un)	to wake (somebody) up
tôt	early
le lendemain	the next day
le lendemain matin	the next morning

SCENE 6: Paris – a conference center

Pierre is now at the conference and meeting Gérard Floret
for the first time. Gérard asks Pierre whether he had a
good flight, whether his hotel is comfortable, and Pierre
tells him the plane was late and he had some trouble
with the hotel night porter. Gérard also asks him how
Catherine is, and goes on to tell Pierre that the conference
has nothing much new to offer. Pierre then spots Jean-Luc
Melville standing by, and seems determined to have a
word with him. Or should one say words ...?

LANGUAGE NOTES

26 **Je déteste les hôtels**
The definite article in French is used very differently from
the way it is used in English. **Le, la, les** is used to refer to a
category of things or people, to things or people in
general.

38 **Je croyais qu'il y avait du nouveau**
Du + adjective in the masculine singular is the construction
corresponding to the English construction *something* +
adjective: *something new* **du nouveau (quelque chose de
nouveau).**

VOCABULARY

un dépliant	leaflet
un portier de nuit	night porter
grave	serious
ça s'est vite arrangé	it soon got sorted out
se plaindre	to complain
ne vous plaignez pas	don't complain
un truc	thing
les vieux trucs	the usual things
du nouveau	something new
devoir	to be supposed to
ils devaient parler	they were supposed to talk
une perte de temps	waste of time
marron	brown
la concurrence	competitor, "the competition"
soutirer (à quelqu'un)	to extract (from somebody)
la suite	what follows, the next scene

Cassette 3   Side 1
Design engineer wanted

SCENE 1: Paris – a conference centre

Pierre is having a word with Jean-Luc Melville, as he intended to do, and accuses him of dishonestly trying to get business information out of him by pretending to be a potential customer. Pierre gets very angry as he goes on and Melville tries to calm him down, saying that if you are in business, this sort of thing is only to be expected. In the end Gérard Floret comes between them and leads Pierre away, suggesting they go and have a drink. Pierre finally goes, but not without a few threatening words to Melville, who seems surprised and quite indignant and is obviously unrepentant. Pierre and Gérard go to a small café nearby which Gérard knows. Pierre relaxes and enjoys being in Paris and being able to sit on a café terrace. They talk about the conference and both agree it has not got much to offer. Neither of them is hungry, but they decide to have another drink, and then to continue their evening somewhere else, to have a few more drinks no doubt ...

LANGUAGE NOTES

11 **Tout en faisant semblant d'être un client**
Tout placed before **en** + **ant** verb form is used to insist on the simultaneity of two actions. In English one would say: *while all the time pretending to be ...*

17 **Je devrais vous casser la figure**
You already know **je dois** *I must.* **Je devrais** is the Conditional form of the same verb, (**devoir**), and means *I should.*

**Qu'est-ce que c'est que toute cette histoire?/Je ne vois
vraiment pas pourquoi**
These two turns of phrase are used by Melville to express
his surprise (real or put on) and his annoyance (*vraiment
pas pourquoi/que toute cette* histoire).

60 **Moi non plus**
You will have recognized this construction, which does
not require a verb in French:
Vous voulez manger quelque chose? Non. Moi non plus.
Do you want to eat something?   No.   Neither do I.

VOCABULARY

un ingénieur d'études	design engineer
la concurrence	the competition
faire semblant	to pretend
faisant semblant	pretending
soutirer	to extract
tout en faisant semblant	while pretending
ne ... que	only
la jungle	jungle
casser la figure (à quelqu'un)	smash (somebody's) face in
faire faillite	to go bankrupt
elle aura fait faillite	it will have gone bankrupt
ne ... plus	no more
vous n'aurez plus de travail	you will have no more work
voir	to see
on verra	we will see
ce n'est pas la peine (de)	it's not worth
prendre un verre	to have a drink
à force de (vouloir)	by, through (wanting)
un état	state
un état pareil	in such a state
franchement	frankly
du temps perdu	a waste of time
faire une de ces têtes	to pull a long face
faillir	to almost do something
j'ai failli (le frapper)	I almost did (hit him)
ça fait du bien de (pouvoir)	it feels good to (be able to)
tant de	so much
incroyable	unbelievable, amazing

EXERCISE 1: Ordering

This practice is meant to help you recognize the sort of
questions you would be asked in a restaurant, and also to
use the right expressions to order what you want. As
usual, try and practise your pronunciation and intonation
a little, as well as paying attention to the vocabulary:
b*iè*re, bout*eille*, bl*o*nde, v*ô*tre,tr*op*, au*jourd*'hui.
Listen carefully to the way words are stressed in
French: the stress falls on the end of the words. And
finally, listen to the different kinds of intonation used
and try to reproduce them as well.

LANGUAGE NOTES

8 **Qu'est-ce que vous *prenez? Je vais prendre* une bière.**
Note that both the Present tense and the immediate future
can be used with no difference in meaning here. The
customer could have answered just as well by saying: **Je
prends une bière.**

22 **Ça fera trente-sept francs**
You already know the phrase **ça fait** to give a *total;* this is
the Future tense of the same verb.

VOCABULARY

commander	to order
quelque chose	something
(une bière) pression	draught (beer)
(une bière) brune	brown (ale)
(une bière) blonde	lager
une glace	ice
un distributeur automatique	(cigarette) machine
(de cigarettes)	
à votre santé	cheers
à la vôtre	cheers

SCENE 2: Paris – the Trans-Infra offices

We find Pierre and Gérard together again, the morning
after ... Both are the worse for wear, especially Pierre,
and Gérard gives him some aspirin and some (rather
puzzling and drastic) advice on how to get rid of his
migraine. After Pierre has taken his aspirin and recovered
a little, he is led to the conference room by a Mr Legrand,
who introduces him to the other people attending. Pierre
is invited to talk about the Geneva project, which he does.
He suggests that they organize regular monthly meetings
of senior design engineers, so that they can exchange and
update information about new techniques in the field of
transport. These meetings would take place in a different
city every month. When he has finished talking, Mr
Legrand voices his objections to the project; the main one
is that he feels he cannot spare his senior design engineer
once a month: he is too busy. He is only prepared to let
one of his younger engineers come to the meetings. Pierre
tries to make him change his mind, but there is nothing
doing it seems ...

LANGUAGE NOTES

19 **Ça m'a l'air dangereux**
M' (me) is the indirect pronoun meaning *to me*. The
phrase means *It seems/looks dangerous to me*. This phrase
is used very often, with all kinds of different adjectives of
course.

35 **En fait nous ne savons rien du tout**
Du tout insists on the idea of *nothing: nothing at all.*

96 **Pas possible? Pourquoi ça?**
The addition of **ça** after **pourquoi** indicates a feeling
of surprise and incredulity. It implies that the person who
is speaking does not really see why something is not
possible, why it can't be done.

115 **autant de temps libre**
Autant de (+ noun) means *that much* or *that many:*
autant d'argent, autant de travail, autant de livres, etc.

VOCABULARY

se sentir (bien)	to feel (well)
comment vous sentez-vous?	how do you feel?
un cachet	tablet
un cachet d'aspirine	an aspirin
faire de l'effet	to work, to have an effect
en bas	down
le sang	blood
la parole	speech
je lui laisse la parole	I'll let him take the floor
dirigé par	run by
consister à	to consist of
un cabinet-conseil	advisory unit
d'occasion	second-hand
un but	aim
potentiel	potential
de notre ressort	our concern, within our scope
se renseigner	to keep/get informed
se réunir	to meet, get together
au sein de	within
se maintenir	to keep (oneself)
de pointe	latest
un niveau	level
de surcroît	in addition
une gamme	range, line
avoir lieu	to take place
par roulement	in rotation
se déplacer	to travel
une réalisation	project
assister à	to attend
s'entendre	to come to an arrangement, agreement
à votre disposition	at your disposal
autant de	as much, as many
libre	free

EXERCISE 2: Explaining a situation

This is a very good exercise to practise remembering language you have just heard and repeating it in a factually and grammatically correct way. As usual, don't forget to pay attention to the pronunciation and the intonation as well.

LANGUAGE NOTES

22 **Nous pourrons *probablement* régler ...**
The place of the adverb in a French sentence can vary, but many of them are placed, as here, after the verb.

25 **Nous pourrons discuter des questions de détail lorsque nous nous réunirons**
Note the use of the Future tense after **lorsque (quand).** In English one would say here: *when we meet again in Paris.*

VOCABULARY

exposer	to explain, explaining
au cours de	during
la suivante	the following, as follows
passionnant	exciting
une fois (par mois)	once (a month)
à nouveau	again

SCENE 3: The Geneva office

We find Pierre in the office, where Liliane, Catherine's assistant, has a message for him from Pascale. She is announcing her imminent arrival in Geneva where she intends to resume her work as Pierre's secretary. Pierre is alarmed at the prospect and asks Liliane whether she knows how to use a telex. Liliane thinks she can manage, so Pierre dictates a message for Pascale, asking her, in brief but unequivocal terms, not to come ... After a slightly bumpy start, Liliane succeeds in sending the message, and Pierre is much happier, and very relieved!

LANGUAGE NOTES

11 **Une certaine Mademoiselle Fontaine**
Note this way of saying *a Miss Fontaine.*

25 **Je pense que oui**
This is the French equivalent of the English *I think so.* The negative form would be: **Je pense que non.**

56 **Attendez que je vous donne des nouvelles**
Another expression followed by a verb in the Subjunctive: **donne** is the first person, Present Subjunctive, of the verb **donner.**

VOCABULARY

de la part de	from
inutile (de)	useless, pointless (to)
auprès de	with
à très bientôt	see you very soon
se servir de	to use
ça marche	it's working
le siège social	head office
occupé	busy, engaged

EXERCISE 3: Describing where things are

This is a fairly easy and straightforward exercise. Listen, repeat and answer, and since the actual contents of this exercise are not difficult, you could perhaps take this opportunity to practise your pronunciation, for instance of words like:

route, droite, quatre, arrière, derrièrc	(r sound);
sur, conductrice, voiture	(u sound);
sous, roues, trouve	(ou sound);
gauche, capot, coffre, d'accord	(different o sounds);
moteur, conducteur, malheureusement	(different eu sounds)
attendant, anglaise, changement, maintenant	(nasal sound an);

Practice makes perfect! ...

VOCABULARY

fameux, fameuse	famous, notorious
indiquer	to indicate, point out
assis	seated, sitting
le conducteur, la conductrice	driver
à droite	on the right
à gauche	on the left
une roue	wheel
à l'avant	at the front
à l'arrière	at the back
sous	underneath
un capot	hood
dans	in
un coffre	trunk
sur	on
une galerie	luggage rack
un toit	roof
un changement de vitesse	gearshift
entre	between
un siège (avant)	(front) seat
derrière	behind
un volant	steering wheel

71

SCENE 4: The Geneva office

Pierre is with Catherine, worrying a lot at the beginning of the scene at the prospect of Pascale turning up in Geneva, should his telex arrive too late. Catherine sympathizes, but confesses that she would not mind meeting this mysterious Pascale ... Pierre goes on to show Catherine a small ad for a post of engineer based in Mexico. He feels like applying: he has not got enough to do and is getting bored and restless. He asks Catherine whether she would be prepared to give him a reference if he applied, and she agrees.

LANGUAGE NOTES

2 **Elle va sans doute arriver**
The adverb comes after the verb it is related to.

27 **J'espère que non**
We saw earlier **Je pense que oui** *I think so*. This is the phrase which means *I hope not*.

J'ai besoin d'avoir quelque chose à faire/Je n'ai pas envie de rester
Vcrb + **de** + Infinitive. Refer to the full list of verbs taking a preposition followed by the Infinitive at the back of your Handbook.

60 **... dans un bureau à ne rien faire**
You have already come across this construction with **à** + Infinitive which is the equivalent of the English turn of phrase: ... *in an office doing nothing*.

63 **Si je posais ma candidature, vous pourriez m'écrire ...?**
Note the sequence of tenses here: the Imperfect tense is used for the first verb, the Conditional for the second. If the first verb was in the Present tense, the second verb would also be in the Present tense, or in the Future tense.

VOCABULARY

parier	to bet
une entrevue	interview
ancien, ancienne (*m.f.*)	old, former
un réseau	network, system
expérimenté	experienced
des équipements	installations
à temps	in time
une petite annonce	small ad
retenu	appointed
mener à bien	to carry through
la réalisation de	the building of
(de) nombreux	numerous
un CCV	curriculum vitae
avoir envie	to want, feel like
je n'ai pas envie (de)	I don't want (to)
vraiment	really
une candidature	application
poser (sa candidature)	to apply (for)
actuel	current
une référence	a reference
une lettre de recommandation	a letter of recommendation
tout de suite	right away

EXERCISE 4: Talking about jobs

There are a lot of very useful terms in this exercise, and you are given different ways of saying the same thing, for you to listen to and reproduce when you give your own answers.

LANGUAGE NOTES

1 **De quoi parlaient-ils? D'un nouveau travail?**
The verb **parler** is followed by the preposition **de** to mean *to talk about something,* which is why these two questions start with **de.**

7 **De quel âge environ?**
De is also used to give someone's age, for instance in expressions such as: **Un garçon de douze ans, un homme de trente ans, une femme de vingt ans.**

11 **Un salaire de treize mille francs**
And **de** is also the preposition used to indicate a price.

29 **Il devra parfois se déplacer**
Note the very irregular Future tense of the verb **devoir** – like other irregular verb forms, you will find it listed in the Grammatical Appendix at the back of this book.

VOCABULARY

du moment que	so long as
un ingénieur électronicien	electronics engineer
un salaire	salary
mensuel	monthly
des conditions de vie (*f.*)	living conditions
une formation (en)	training, background (in)
passer une annonce	to put an ad in the paper
un site touristique	tourist spot, sight

SCENE 5: The Geneva office

In this scene Pierre is giving Catherine an account of his visit to Paris. It is a very gloomy one: he tells her that everything was a disaster, from his arrival at the hotel to the conference itself and, even worse, the committee meeting. He explains to Catherine how Mr Legrand won't part with his senior engineer once a month. Catherine obviously knows Legrand and decides to sort things out straight away. She phones Xavier Dumur and tells him how things are with Legrand. Dumur seems to agree with Catherine that this is not acceptable and advises her to speak to Legrand directly, which she does. She simply "asks" Legrand to send his senior engineer to Geneva on the 3rd, and to make sure that he has his passport and a seat on the plane for that date. Pierre is suitably impressed by Catherine's authority and competence. He invites her to have dinner with him, but she declines.

LANGUAGE NOTES

15 **Le pire, c'est qu'il ne s'est rien passé non plus ...**
You have already come across many instances of this turn of phrase. Similarly, one can also say: **le mieux, c'est que ..., le plus intéressant, c'est que ..., le plus drôle, c'est que ...**, etc. There is another example of this sort of construction in this scene: ***Tout ce que* nous pouvons obtenir de Paris, *c'est* un jeune ingénieur.**

30 **Un blond, mince**
Here the adjective **blond** is used as a noun; it is equivalent of **un homme blond, mince.**

36 **Pour faire des difficultés, ça, il s'y connaît**
This is a familiar way of stressing one's disapproval of someone or someone's behaviour: *He certainly knows how to be awkward/how to make difficulties.*

44 **Pourrais-je parler à M. Dumur?**
This formal way of framing a question is often used on the phone when asking to speak to someone.

46 C'est Catherine à l'appareil
This is the French way of saying *This is Catherine
speaking.* **L'appareil** in question is of course the
telephone! When one wants to know who is phoning, the
phrase used is **Qui est à l'appareil?**

47 Nous, ça va, mais pas le travail
An interesting construction here: **ça** refers to **nous,** and
the full form would be: **Nous, nous allons bien.** Also note
the non-verbal phrase: **mais pas le travail;** understood:
mais le travail, lui, ne va pas.

73 Qu'est-ce que vous en dites?
En here means *about it, of it: what do you think of it/about
it?*

VOCABULARY

épouvantable	appalling
qu'est-ce qui n'a pas marché?	what went wrong?
infect	terrible, filthy
le pire	the worst (thing)
un débutant	beginner
un stagiaire	traincc
mince	slim
pénible	painful, a pain
il s'y connaît	he's an expert, he knows all about that
régler	to sort out, solve
ça ne vous dérange pas si ...?	do you mind if ...?
un ingénieur expert	engineering specialist
soutenir	to support
tout bonnement	quite simply
impressionnant	impressive
tant pis	too bad

EXERCISE 5: Reporting events

As usual, listen and take part when you feel you are
ready. Pay attention to the use of tenses in this practice.

LANGUAGE NOTES

**Nous sommes allés à Paris/Nous sommes descendus dans
un petit hôtel/Nous avons visité les sites touristiques/Nous
sommes rentrés dimanche**
The Perfect tense is used a lot in this practice to refer to a
succession of actions which took place in the past.

**L'hôtel était très agréable/Les petits déjeuners étaient très
bons/C'était très intéressant**
The Imperfect tense on the other hand is used to
describe someone, something or a state of mind as in **Je
voulais.** (As we have seen before, it is also used to refer to
something which used to happen regularly in the past, or
to refer to something which was in the course of
happening.)

VOCABULARY

rapporter	to report, reporting
un événement	event
savoir	to know how to, to be able to
je saurais	I would be able (to)
en faire autant	to do the same
descendre dans (un hôtel)	stay at (a hotel)
nous sommes descendus	we stayed
faire la connaissance (de)	to meet, get to know
falloir	to be necessary
il a fallu que nous fassions connaissance	we had to meet
eux	them
se revoir	to meet again
des sites touristiques	the (tourist) sights
la suite	the next part

SCENE 6: The Geneva office

Pierre is coming to see Catherine in her office. When she
sees him, she suddenly remembers that he wanted her to
write a reference for him, and she apologizes for not
having done it. Pierre, however, is still trying to get
Catherine to have dinner with him, or at least a drink. As
they are discussing the possibilities, they are interrupted
by Liliane who has come to tell Catherine that Alain
Tanner has already phoned three times, but Catherine
was not there. Liliane then proceeds to repeat in detail
Alain Tanner's message: that he has found a very good
new restaurant where they could go together, that he
would like her to wear the same dress as on the previous
Saturday ... The phone rings again, so Catherine answers.
While she is on the phone (Liliane thinks it must be
Tanner again) Liliane gives a detailed account to Pierre of
Catherine's relationship with Tanner and its progress. We
sense through Pierre's short replies that he is getting
somewhat annoyed ... But Catherine soon comes back
with some sensational news: it wasn't Alain Tanner on the
phone, after all ...

LANGUAGE NOTES

12 **Vous vouliez me parler?**
Note the use of the Imperfect tense here. This is just a
variation on the Present tense form: *did you want to talk
to me?*

31 **Qu'est-ce qu'il y a?**
Here, this means *What is the matter?*

72 **C'était elle au téléphone**   *It was her on the phone.*
Elle is also the stressed form of the pronoun. For the
masculine, the form is **lui.**

VOCABULARY

pas spécialement	not particularly
rien ne presse	there's no hurry
sans faute	without fail
c'est dommage	it's a pity
meilleur	better
ça ne fait rien	it doesn't matter
retrouver	to meet, see
il vous retrouvera chez vous	he'll see you at your place
celui, celle (*m.f.*)	the one
voir	to see
voyons	let's see

Cassette 3   Side 2
Now, Frankfurt

SCENE 1: Geneva – a café

Pierre is sitting in a café in Geneva when Catherine finds
him, very nervous and worried as to Pascale's movements
and whereabouts. Catherine attempts to calm him down
over a drink and finally manages to tell him that Pascale is
still in Strasbourg. She phoned from the airport:
Catherine told her that Pierre was leaving soon for
Mexico and that there was therefore no point in
her coming. Pierre is naturally very relieved on
hearing this and invites Catherine to have another drink to
celebrate the good news. But Catherine has to go, so
Pierre orders another beer for himself.

LANGUAGE NOTES

20 **Ça ne sert à rien de s'énerver**
This is a frequently used construction:
Ça ne sert à rien de + Infinitive.

64 **Vous m'avez sauvé la vie**
Note this construction, and the use of the personal
pronoun, **me (m').** Compare with English: *You saved my
life.*

71 **Qu'est-ce que c'est, déjà, le prénom de M. Tanner?**
Another emphatic turn of phrase, where **ça (c')** stresses
the real subject of **être: le prénom de M. Tanner.**
Déjà is often used when you have forgotten a piece of
information and want to be told again. Here, the question
implies that Pierre used to know Mr. Tanner's first name
but can't remember it.

81 **Je peux avoir encore un demi ...?**
Another way of asking for something. You already know
several: **je voudrais, j'aimerais, pourrais-je?** for instance.
This one, **je peux ...?,** is used all the time in spoken
French.

VOCABULARY

un demi	a half (pint of beer)
frais	cool
commander	to order
il commandera	he will order
se cacher	to hide
vous vous cachez	you are hiding
ça ne sert à rien de	there's no point
s'énerver	to get annoyed
un jus d'orange	orange juice
mettez-vous à ma place	put yourself in my shoes
se rendre compte	to realize
elle ne se rend pas compte	she doesn't realize
Grands dieux!	Goodness! Gracious!
la vérité	truth
empêcher	to prevent
vous avez empêché	you prevented
ce n'est pas la peine de	it's not worth
génial	great, brilliant
quel poids en moins	that's a weight off my mind
se détendre	to relax
fêter	to celebrate
reprendre	to have another
vous reprenez quelque chose	do you want something else to drink?
un prénom	first name, christian name
sauver la vie (à quelqu'un)	to save somebody's life
vous m'avez sauvé la vie	you saved my life

EXERCISE 1: Reported speech

This exercise gives you the opportunity to practise at length the change from direct speech to reported speech and the change of tenses involved.

LANGUAGE NOTES

4 **Ma propre langue**
Propre is the word used to insist on the idea of possession.

6 **Je fais ça tout le temps/... je voudrais voir si je peux le faire**
Ça and **le** are used to refer to an action previously mentioned: **répétait à Catherine sa conversation téléphonique,** in this sentence.

14 **Il viendra jeudi**
No preposition necessary in French to indicate the day of the week. Again, note how **jeudi** can mean *next* (or *the coming*) *Thursday,* when used with the Future tense. If used with the Past tense, it would mean *last Thursday.*

24 **Je crois comprendre**
The verb **croire** can be followed by **que** + a full sentence, or, as here, by just an Infinitive if it is the same person who performs both the actions described by the verbs.

VOCABULARY

les paroles	words
rapporter les paroles de quelqu'un	saying what somebody else has said
envoyer	to send
vous enverriez	you would send

SCENE 2: The Geneva office

Françoise has arrived and Catherine is showing her
around after explaining that Pierre is in Frankfurt.
Catherine tells Françoise about the committee meeting
and what she will have to do. Then she introduces her to
the people who work in the office and shows her where
everything is. She leaves her to get used to the place and
the people before they start work in about an hour's time.

LANGUAGE NOTES

8 **Vous n'avez pas eu de difficultés? Non, aucune.**
Aucun, aucune means *none*. Here it is **aucune** because it
refers to the feminine word **difficultés.**

10 **J'ai mis un quart d'heure pour venir ...**
Make a note of this way of saying how to do
something.

Ça viendra/Il faudra faire attention
Two more very irregular verbs in the Future tense, **venir**
and **faire.** All the irregular forms are listed in the
Appendix.

Tout le monde doit avoir une chambre d'hôtel/... un aide-
comptable et un informaticien qui doivent commencer la
semaine prochaine
An illustration of the two meanings of **devoir:** 1) *must,* in
the first sentence, 2) *to be supposed to,* in the second.

82 **Vous êtes la directrice**
The definite article is used here to mean *the manager of*
this particular company.

VOCABULARY

mettre	to take (time)
j'ai mis un quart d'heure	it took me a quarter of an hour
retenir	to remember
se rendre à	to go to
des gens	the people
bon, bons (*sing., pl.*)	right, correct
les bons dossiers (*m.*)	the right files
la routine	routine
un directeur	manager, director
le service comptable	marketing department
un comptable	accountant
un aide-comptable	accountant's assistant, book-keeper
un informaticien	computer scientist (man)
jeter un coup d'œil	have a (quick) look
j'ai déjà jeté un coup d'œil	I've already had a quick look
des fournitures (*f.*)	stationery
s'habituer	to get used to
environ	about, roughly

EXERCISE 2: Showing someone around

This is a useful exercise to put into practice the vocabulary you have learned, and to practice changing pronouns, asking and answering precise questions.

LANGUAGE NOTES

8 **C'est celui-là votre bureau**
Note this way of showing something to someone, pointing to it to indicate it is theirs; similarly, one will say: **c'est celle-là sa table, c'est celui-là ton livre, c'est celle-là sa machine à écrire.**

33 **Et où est-ce que je peux le trouver, l'aide-comptable?**
The direct object complement is stressed here, with the help of the pronoun **le.**

VOCABULARY

faire visiter (quelqu'un)	to show (somebody) around
un placard	cupboard
un crayon	pencil
se familiariser avec	to get used to, familiarize oneself with
la routine	routine
le courrier	mail
trier (le courrier)	to sort (the mail)
voisin	next to

85

SCENE 3: Frankfurt airport and Herr Runde's office

At the beginning of the scene, Pierre is phoning Herr Runde from the airport to let him know that he is coming in a taxi, having failed to find Herr Runde's secretary at the airport. We find him again with Herr Runde. They talk for a while about airports and wonder what can have happened to Sophie. Herr Runde seems fairly confident that she will come back one day ... Pierre then asks Herr Runde whether it will be possible for him to speak in French at the conference. Herr Runde says yes, provided Pierre speaks slowly and clearly. Pierre says he can always manage in English if necessary. They talk about how long the meeting is likely to last and Herr Runde asks Pierre whether he needs anything for his talk, but Pierre has everything he needs. Then Pierre asks Herr Runde if he could have a look at what they do, and Herr Runde agrees to take him round.

LANGUAGE NOTES

13 **Vous avez bien fini par trouver le chemin!**
We see here how important prepositions are, and how they can slightly modify the meaning of a verb. Compare:
Il a fini de travailler.   *He has finished working.*
Il a (bien) fini par travailler!   *He finally ended up working!*
                                       He DID work in the end!

19 **... quand elle en aura assez de me chercher**
Note the tense used here after **quand** in French: it is followed by the Future tense, whereas in English the Perfect tense is used: *when she has had enough of looking for me.*

Si vous vous trompez ..., vous pouvez très bien attendre .../ S'il y avait des problèmes ..., je pourrais toujours parler ...
Two examples of the sequence of tenses after **si.**

59 **Je vous ferai visiter**
Faire + verb in the Infinitive corresponds to the English construction *to have (someone) do (something), to make (someone) do (something).* Literally, the above sentence means: *I will make you visit.*

63 J'ai tout ce qu'il me faut

This is the French sentence meaning *I have everything I need* (literally: *I have everything which I need*).

VOCABULARY

inquiet (pour)	worried (about)
en avoir assez de	to be fed up with
quand elle en aura assez de (chercher)	when she's fed up with (looking)
finir par (trouver)	to finally manage (to find)
un point de rencontre	meeting place, assembly point
se tromper de (rendez-vous)	to get (the meeting place) wrong
pas grand'chose	not much
sans doute	probably
lentement	slowly
clairement	clearly
se débrouiller	to manage
durer	to last
au courant	up-to-date, informed
relever	to underline, stress

EXERCISE 3: Arranging to meet someone

This exercise gives you an opportunity to practise both question forms and prepositions – such as **par (par le train), à (à la gare, à la sortie, au restaurant), vers (vers trois heures et demie), sous (sous la pendule).**

LANGUAGE NOTES

20 **Et si le train a du retard?**
Note this way of saying that *the train is running late.*
You may already know the phrase **être en retard,** which is used for people. For trains, buses, planes, etc., the phrase used is **avoir du retard:**
Je suis en retard parce que mon train avait du retard.

34 **Je vous retrouve vers trois heures et demie**
The Present tense is used to make an appointment for the near future.

VOCABULARY

une pendule	clock
une sortie	exit

SCENE 4: Frankfurt – a conference room

Pierre is addressing the conference and explaining the regular meetings planned between engineers of different nationalities. He proposes four topics for discussion at these meetings. When he has finished, Herr Runde offers him coffee and then takes him around the factory. After the visit Herr Runde invites Pierre to have a drink with him in the evening and offers to take him sightseeing around Frankfurt. At the end of the scene they are on their way to the design department.

LANGUAGE NOTES

8 **Nous nous sommes installés à Genève récemment**
Reflexive verbs have a Past Participle which agrees with
the subject of the verb in the Past tense, as all reflexive
verbs are conjugated with **être**.

**... pour que des réunions aient lieu régulièrement/
Il est essentiel que nous les connaissions**
Note the use of the Subjunctive here, after **pour que** and
the set phrase **Il est essentiel que.**

VOCABULARY

malheureusement	unfortunately
s'installer	to move to
nous nous sommes installés	we've opened an office
récemment	recently
se dérouler	to take place
successivement	in succession
une rubrique	heading, category
un matériel	equipment, hardware
la locomotion	transport
la réalisation	development
un moteur	motor, engine
une voie	track
des équipements routiers	road systems
l'assemblage (*m.*)	assembly
la programmation	programming
le minutage	timing
un système informatique	computer (system)
magnétique	magnetic
pneumatique	pneumatic
naître	to be born
ils naissent	they are born
le bureau d'études	design department
un atelier	workshop
la puissance	strength, power
une chaîne de montage	assembly-line
un lot	batch, consignment

EXERCISE 4: Asking people out

In this exercise you are given a chance to remember and practise various polite forms of invitation, and polite answers to them. Listen and practise, paying attention to the intonation.

LANGUAGE NOTES

20 ... **parce qu'elle ne peut pas y aller**
Remember that **y** must not be left out in French, as *there* is in English: *because she can't go.*

VOCABULARY

désolé	sorry
avoir peur	to be afraid
elle a peur	she's afraid
inviter	to invite
une invitation	an invitation
regretter	to regret

SCENE 5: The Geneva office

Pierre is now back at the office. There he finds Françoise, who has started work, and he asks her whether she is settling in and whether there are any problems. She says she still needs a little time but she is fine and there are no problems at all. She asks Pierre if he had a good trip to Frankfurt and when he came back. Pierre then wants to know if Catherine is in her office and if she is busy. Françoise says she is free and Pierre goes in. Catherine asks about Frankfurt and Pierre gives her a detailed account of their decisions about the next meeting, and of the program which they established. But Françoise interrupts them with an urgent and mysterious message: she has got something on the telex which should interest Pierre and Catherine greatly ...

LANGUAGE NOTES

29 **Vous savez si elle est occupée?**
Indirect question , using **si.** The direct question would
be: **Est-ce qu'elle est occupée?**

31 **Il n'y a personne avec elle**
Note this expression meaning literally: *there isn't
anyone* or *there is nobody.*

50 **Nous ne serons que quatre, ce qui est très bien**
Ce qui is used here to sum up the whole of the previous
sentence: *There will only be the four of us, which is very
good.*

51 **... une petite commission est beaucoup plus efficace qu'une
grande**
Beaucoup is used here to emphasize the comparative:
much more effective than a big one.

VOCABULARY

s'installer	to settle in
vous vous installez	you're settling in
s'adapter (à)	to adapt (to)
jusqu'à présent	up to now
plutôt ... que	rather ... than
efficace	efficient
l'ordre du jour	agenda
établir un programme	to set up a program
une prévision	forecast
à venir	to come
la faisabilité	feasibility
une évaluation	evaluation
centralisé(e)	centralised
impressionnant	impressive
interrompre	to interrupt

EXERCISE 5: Making small talk

This is a vocabulary exercise to help you use all the
questions and answers which make up polite conversation,
especially when enquiring whether someone had a good
journey. As the contents are quite straightforward, you
could concentrate on the pronunciation of a few words
and sounds, for instance:
– all the nasal sounds, in:
     attendant/quelqu'un/bon/
     Londres/reviens/long/fatigant
– the difference between these sounds:
    u   sur/revenue   and **ou**   trouvé/beaucoup

LANGUAGE NOTES

22 **On est très fatigué en arrivant**
    Use of **on** once again to mean *one, people.*

VOCABULARY

se passer	to happen, take place
comment s'est passé le voyage?	how did the journey go?
poli	polite
la politesse	politeness
anodin	trivial, harmless
agréable	pleasant
épuisant	exhausting
fascinant	fascinating
fatigant	tiring

SCENE 6: The Geneva office

Françoise shows Pierre and Catherine the message which has just come up on the telex. It comes from Cairo. The Egyptians want to build a completely new town, and they need a complete design, starting from scratch and taking it through to the finished product. The Egyptian Minister of Planning is arriving the following day. Catherine has met him before when they were working together on a project in Alexandria. She is fairly confident that they will get the contract. Pierre has to be present at the meeting as well. He too is sure that they will get the contract, as according to him they can offer better prices, they are more competent and their delivery service is the best. The phone rings, and Françoise answers: it is Alain Tanner, inviting Catherine to go out with him. But she tells him very firmly that she can't, and that he had better not ring her again, as they have nothing further to say to each other. Pierre and Catherine then resume their conversation; Françoise is going to call the hotel where the minister is staying, and also let Olivier and Jean-Pierre know that there is a meeting the following day. Pierre for his part mentions to Catherine the fact that he has overheard her conversation on the phone and makes sympathetic noises. But Catherine does not seem to be unduly upset by it all, and ends up in fact by reminding Pierre that he invited her to dinner some time ago, and by asking him if HE is busy that evening ...

LANGUAGE NOTES

18   **Il arrive ce soir**
Another example of the Present tense being used to refer to the near future.

32   **Nous quatre**
The combination of pronoun + number is the equivalent of the English the + number + of + pronoun:

nous cinq	*the five of us*
vous deux	*the two of you*
eux trois	*the three of them*

51 **Acceptez-le**
Le *it,* refers to things as they stand, to the facts that
Catherine has just explained to Alain.

71 **Je suis désolé que les choses n'aillent plus très bien ...**
Another expression followed by the Subjunctive: **être
désolé que.**

VOCABULARY

les moyens de transport	means of transport
une étude	study
la grandeur	size
la Planification	Planning
obtenir	to obtain
vous obtiendrez	you will obtain
cirer	to polish
pas grand'chose	not much
de toute façon	in any case
après-vente	after the sale
un délai	deadline
une livraison	delivery
décrocher (un contrat)	to win, land (a contract)
franchement	frankly
avertir	to warn
une rupture	break-up (relationship)
prévoir	to plan
prévu	planned, foreseen

Cassette 4   Side 1
Mexico

SCENE 1: The Geneva office

Jean-Pierre and Olivier have just heard about the
Egyptian project and are very pleased. They discuss with
Catherine the time and place of their meeting in the
morning. Then Catherine leaves and Olivier and Jean-
Pierre talk about the Egyptian project and discuss what
their chances are of getting the contract. Jean-Pierre
explains how it is sometimes possible to find ways around
the laws governing the advertising of public bidding,
which isn't always as public as it seems to be ... It is
easy in fact to decide in advance who is going to get the
contract, and to give them plenty of time to present a
project, and not enough time to the other applicants.
Everyone agrees that at this stage there is not much
they can do, but Olivier still wants to have another look at
the accounts. Catherine who has come back to the office
reminds Pierre of their dinner appointment before finally
leaving, having told Olivier not to work too late. Olivier
and Jean-Pierre then proceed to make fun of Pierre for
taking "the boss" out to dinner, and advise him to go
home and get changed, not forgetting the after-shave!

LANGUAGE NOTES

7   **... et qu'on part pour l'hôtel à la demie**
La demie is an abbreviation of the full time when it is
obvious what time one is referring to, here **neuf heures et
demie.** Similarly, one talks about **le quart, moins le quart,
moins dix,** etc.

Ça veut dire/ça signifie
Two verbs meaning the same: *it/that means.*

Attends./Tu passes .../Tu ajoutes .../Tu vois?
You will have noticed that Olivier and Jean-Pierre say **tu**
to Pierre too, but all say **vous** to Catherine and she says
vous back to them, although she is in the same age group
as they are. This is partly because some of them have not
known her that long, or she them, but also it is because
she is their boss.

Les offres publiques ne sont pas toujours aussi publiques que ça/Mais si, elles doivent l'être, obligatoirement
1) **aussi** + adjective + **que: aussi publiques que ça** would be rendered in English as *as public as that.*
2) **Mais si: si** is used instead of **oui** to give an affirmative answer to a negative question.

76 **Comment ça?**
This is the question used when someone wishes something to be explained further to them.

91 **C'est pas très honnête, tout ça/C'est comme ça, les affaires**
In everyday spoken French the first part of the negation **(ne)** is very often dropped. Also note here once again how **c'est** is used to stress a group of words in the sentence, here **tout ça** and **les affaires.**

110 **Il y en a vraiment de très astucieux**
Il y en a + **de** + adjective. This construction is frequently used.

132 **Qu'est-ce que tu as?**
In this context, this sentence means *what's the matter with you?/what's wrong with you?*

135 **Alors, qui est-ce qui invite la patronne à dîner?**
This type of question, **qui est-ce qui** being used here instead of just **qui,** is used because the intention is ironic or sarcastic. In other words it is not a "real" question, but a sarcastic comment. The English equivalent would be *So who's inviting the boss to dinner?*

144 **A toi de jouer, Pierre**
C'est is not always expressed in this type of phrase. Similarly, in an earlier passage, instead of **C'est à nous de nous débrouiller,** one could have said **A nous de nous débrouiller.**

VOCABULARY

faire photocopier (quelque chose)	to have (something) photocopied
falloir	to have to
il faudra bien	we will have to
tôt ou tard	sooner or later
suffire	to be enough, sufficient
il suffit que nous soyons	we just need to be
aimable	friendly, pleasant
une offre publique	public bidding (on a contract)
soumissioner	to bid
une loi	law
tourner	to get around
un appel d'offres	request for bids, bids wanted
lequel, lesquels (*sing., pl.*)	which?
soumettre	to submit
en sorte que	so that
parvenir (à)	to reach
elles ne leur parviennent pas	they don't reach them
la clôture	closing
exécuter	to carry out, complete
astucieux	shrewd, clever
bête	silly
louche	dubious, 'fishy'
se faire à (quelque chose)	to get used to (something)
il faut s'y faire	you have to get used to it
confier l'affaire	to award the contract
un chiffre	figure
contourner	to get around
un entrepreneur	contractor
réussir	to succeed
des affaires (*f.*)	business
rompre	to break off (relationship)
elle a rompu avec lui	she's broken off with him

EXERCISE 1: Possibilities

This is a useful practice to help you remember the meaning of different words which appeared in the corresponding scene. It also enables you to use the construction with **si** and to practise using the right tense.

LANGUAGE NOTES

11 **Ils veulent que des sociétés fassent une offre**
You will remember that after the verb **vouloir** the Subjunctive is required.

20 **N'importe qui peut faire une offre?**
N'importe qui means *anybody,* and is followed by a verb in the third person singular.

VOCABULARY

une chance	a chance
un succès	success
obtenir	to obtain
un hangar	hangar
participer (à)	to take part (in)
décrocher (un contrat)	to land, to get (a contract)
la compétence	competence
requis(e)	requested

SCENE 2: Geneva – in a restaurant

In this scene we see Pierre and Catherine in a restaurant, ordering a meal. Pierre is rather disappointed to find out that one can only dance on Fridays and Saturdays. When they order the meal, Pierre wants to eat something hot, and is worried that he is not going to have enough to eat. He is very hungry. The waiter, having come round once and gone, comes back and takes their order. Pierre asks him whether he will have enough to eat. The waiter assures him that portions are very generous, but that if Pierre is still hungry he can always order an extra portion. Catherine orders venison, but there isn't any, so the waiter offers some alternative dishes ...

LANGUAGE NOTES

10 **le vendredi et le samedi**
This means *every Friday and every Saturday.*

16 **Si vous y tenez vraiment**
The verb is **tenir à (quelque chose),** so **y** replaces
à danser. Similarly, one will say **Pensez-y** *(think about it),*
with the verb **penser à.**

24 **Avocat aux crevettes**
The preposition **à** sometimes means **avec. Aux** here means
avec des. Similarly, a few lines further on, you have **soufflé
aux asperges.**

VOCABULARY

un cabaret	cabaret/nightclub
un dancing	dance hall
zut!	shoot!
tenir à (faire quelque chose)	to insist (on doing something)
si vous y tenez	if you really want to
un avocat	avocado
une crevette	shrimp
chaud, chaude *(m.f.)*	warm
une asperge	asparagus
le gibier	game
du chevreuil	venison
avoir faim	to be hungry
vraiment	really
un supplément	extra portion
minuscule	minute
se battre	to fight
deux pommes de terre qui se battent	two potatoes fighting
une carré d'agneau	loin of lamb
une écrevisse	crayfish
raisonnable	reasonable
copieux	generous, copious
une portion	portion
supplémentaire	extra

EXERCISE 2: Ordering a meal

In this exercise you are given the opportunity to practise all the questions and phrases used to order a meal in a restaurant and the vocabulary used to describe the food being served. Listen and then fill in the gaps with your answers, remembering if you can to pay attention to the intonation.

LANGUAGE NOTES

4 **Comment est-ce qu'on appelle le garçon?**
Note this idiomatic way of asking what something is called, using **on.**

11 **Je vous apporte un menu**
In French the plain Present tense is used to refer to something which is going to be done in the minutes which follow one's statement. The English equivalent would be: *I'll bring you a menu.*

17 **Et comme légumes?**
A different use of **comme** here, meaning *for, as, in the way of.* Earlier on in the Course, you had another example of this, with the question **Qu'est-ce que vous faites comme métier?**

25 **Donnez-moi un Côtes-du-Rhône, s'il vous plaît**
There are several examples of polite requests in this scene, for instance:
> **Je voudrais voir ...**
> **Je peux avoir ...?**
But you see that it is polite enough to say **donnez-moi,** in the Imperative, provided one uses **s'il vous plaît** with it. Also note the use of the article **un** before the name of the wine.

43 **Maintenant qu'ils ont fini de dîner**   *Now that they have finished dinner.*

VOCABULARY

un chateaubriand	chateaubriand (large fillet steak)
à point	medium
des petits pois (*m.*)	(green) peas
la salade	green salad
une entrée	starter
le porto	port
comme boisson?	(what would you like) to drink?
l'addition (*f.*)	bill
le garçon	waiter
un dessert	dessert
délicieux	delicious

SCENE 3: Geneva – in Pierre's car

In this short scene Pierre is taking Catherine home. She thanks him for the evening, for the meal and the drink they had in a little bar afterwards. Pierre offers to take her to have a last drink in another bar, but Catherine declines, saying that she wants to be fit, not too tired, in the morning. Pierre tries to get himself invited in for a cup of coffee, but Catherine obviously does not wish things to go too far for the moment, and says they'd better not have a coffee together at this late hour. Pierre then suggests that they go out together the following evening, but Catherine is very non-commital. They say good night and Pierre leaves.

LANGUAGE NOTES

... il est temps que je rentre/... désolée que vous n'ayez pas pu danser
Two more expressions followed by a verb in the Subjunctive. **Ayez pu** is the Past Subjunctive of the verb **pouvoir.**

31 **Je ne voudrais pas que nous nous fâchions**
You already know **je voudrais** followed by a verb in the Infinitive when the same person is the subject of both verbs. For example: **Je ne voulais pas me fâcher.** When **je voudrais** and the verb which follows refer to actions performed by different persons, one has to use **que** + a verb in the Subjunctive, as here.

32 **Si nous sortions demain soir?**
Si followed by the Imperfect tense is used to make a suggestion, to issue an informal invitation to someone to do something.

33 **On verra**
This is the phrase used when one does not wish to commit oneself to doing something or agreeing to something, or when one is not sure what is in store for the future.

VOCABULARY

être en forme	to be fit, to be in good shape
il ne vaut mieux pas	(I'd) better not
entraîner	to lead
(cela) pourrait nous entraîner vers autre chose	one thing could lead to another
quel mal y a-t-il à ça?	what's wrong with that?
en vouloir à quelqu'un	to bear a grudge against somebody
vous ne m'en voulez pas	you don't hold it against me
se fâcher	to get angry
voir	to see
je vous verrai	I'll see you
bonne nuit	goodnight

EXERCISE 3: Saying goodbye

This is a useful exercise that goes over the different expressions of thanks and the friendly ways of taking leave of someone. As usual, particularly because the vocabulary and grammatical contents of the exercise do not present any difficulty, take this opportunity to pay special attention to the pronunciation and intonation.

LANGUAGE NOTES

6 **Je vous verrai demain?/On se voit demain?**
The use of **on** introduces/implies an element of familiarity.

20 **C'est le matin où Catherine et toute l'équipe vont rencontrer ...**
In French **où** is used here, whereas in English one would say *It is the morning when ...*

VOCABULARY

le lendemain	the next day
demain	tomorrow
plaire (à)	to please
est-ce que la soirée lui a plu?	did he enjoy the evening?
dormir	to sleep
dormez bien	sleep well
une équipe (*f.*)	team

SCENE 4: The Geneva office and Mr Chahine's hotel

Everyone gathers in the office ready to leave for the hotel. Jean-Pierre is very keen to learn from Pierre what happened the previous evening with Catherine but Pierre refuses to co-operate. Catherine arrives; her car is a little small for four people, so Jean-Pierre offers to take Olivier with him, and Pierre can take Catherine in his car. When they arrive at the hotel, Catherine phones Mohamed in his room to let him know they have arrived, and they go up. Mohamed is very pleased to see Catherine, whom he has not seen for at least five years, and she introduces her three colleagues to him. He invites everyone to come in and sit down, and orders coffee for six.

LANGUAGE NOTES

11 **Oh, ne recommence pas, hein!**
Hein! at the end of an Imperative sentence like this is an expression of impatience, exasperation or even threat.

51 **Ça fait longtemps que je ne vous ai pas vue.** *It is a long time since I last saw you.*
Make a note of this construction, which is very frequently used in French. Instead of **Ça fait,** one could have **Il y a.**

53 **Ça doit faire au moins cinq ans**
Devoir indicates probability here; **faire** is used to indicate a total.

52 **Oh, appelez-moi Mohamed**
Although the Imperative is used, this is a friendly invitation by Mohamed to the others to call him by his first name: *Oh, do call me Mohamed.*

VOCABULARY

raconter	to tell
raconte-moi	tell me all about it
un patron, une patronne	boss
tarder	to be long
nous n'allons pas tarder à partir	we'll be leaving soon
proposer	to suggest
je te propose une chose	I suggest this
emmener	to take (*by car*)
nous y sommes	here (there) we are
intérieur	internal
etage	floor
ça fait longtemps que je ne vous ai pas vue	it's a long time since I last saw you
devoir	must
ça doit faire	it must be
amener	to bring (*for people*)
vous avez amené?	have you brought?
apporter	to bring (*for objects*)

EXERCISE 4: Meeting old friends

An exercise which enables you to practise various
ways of making conversation with someone you meet
again after a long time. It also shows you clearly how to
change from direct to indirect speech.

LANGUAGE NOTES

27 **Si longtemps que ça?**
Si or **aussi** + adjective/adverb + **que** + **ça** is
the sentence pattern corresponding to the English
construction *as … as that.*

34 **Bien sûr, je m'en souviens**
En is the pronoun used with a verb which takes the
preposition **de: se souvenir de,** therefore **je m'en souviens.**
When the verb takes the preposition **à,** the pronoun used is **y:**
   penser à,   therefore: **j'y pense.**

VOCABULARY

rencontrer	to meet
une connaissance	acquaintance, person you know
ressembler (à quelqu'un)	to look like (somebody)
elle ressemble trait pour trait à	she's the spitting image of
faire signe (à quelqu'un)	to wave, make a sign (to somebody)
elle te fait signe	she's waving to you
rectifier	to correct
devenir	to become (of)
ce qu'il devient	what he's doing now, how he's been
qu'est-ce que tu deviens?	what has become of you? how has life been with you?
depuis	since
tant mieux	great, I'm glad to hear it
se passer	to take place
comment se passe (la négociation)	how the negotiations are going

SCENE 5: Geneva – Mr Chahine's suite

The meeting between Catherine and her colleagues and Mohamed Chahine – Jean-Pierre is explaining to Mohamed the many advantages of the system they have got to offer. Mohamed wants to know whether the administrative side of things will take a long time to settle, but Catherine assures him that the four of them can deal with everything very rapidly. Jean-Pierre adds that they can afford to choose, which is why their prices are so competitive. Mohamed is impressed, and wishes to know when they can present him with a detailed bid. Catherine thinks it will take about eight to ten weeks, and suggests they prepare two or three alternative projects. She points out that her team will need to know the cost of fuel, what system of electricity they have, etc. Catherine also gives Mohamed to understand that she and her team do not wish to do all this work for nothing, and tries to get him to tell her whether they are likely to get the contract in the end. Mohamed answers that they have asked three companies to prepare offers, that Catherine's chances are good but that he cannot promise anything more precise. However, his last remarks to Catherine lead us to think that things might go her way ...

LANGUAGE NOTES

11 **En commençant maintenant ...**
En + Present Participle indicates simultaneity between two actions; it also expresses the means of doing something: *By starting now ...*

14 **... en même temps que vous dessinez le plan de la ville**
En même temps que means *at the same time as* and indicates simultaneity between two actions.

52 **... une idée du budget dont vous disposez**
Dont is the relative pronoun used, to mean *of whom, of which, whose,* with verbs which take the preposition **de** after them.

53 Combien nous voulons déposer?
When one wants time to think up an answer to a question,
or to confirm what the other person said, one
sometimes repeats the question, formulating it in a
different way. Note the word order with **combien: vous
voulez savoir** is understood here: **Vous voulez savoir
combien nous voulons dépenser?**

**Le mieux, c'est de faire un descriptif .../Ça, je ne peux pas
vous le dire**
Two more examples of an emphatic turn of phrase: note
again the wide use of **ça** in everyday conversation.

VOCABULARY

une suite	(hotel) suite
faire ses preuves	to prove itself
(il) a fait ses preuves	it's tried and true
fonctionner (à)	to work (by)
ça fonctionner à l'électricité	it's electrically powered
la place	space
l'espace (*m.*)	room, space
disposer (de)	to have at one's disposal
nous disposons de beaucoup d'espace	we have a lot of room
éviter	to avoid
dresser	to draw up
faire appel à	to call upon
le monde (du monde)	world (in the world)
un point de vue	point of view
être	to be
nous sommes (quatre)	there are (four) of us
se faire	to be done
tout peut se faire	everything can be dealt with
avantageux	attractive (price)
bénéficier (de)	to benefit from
nous en faisons bénéficier le client	we pass on the benefits to the customer
une ébauche	sketch, outline
un accord	agreement
une ébauche d'accord	an outline agreement

dépenser	to spend
un descriptif	outline
un coût	cost
la consommation	consumption
le prix de revient	cost
la main-d'œuvre	labour
là-dessus	about that
voir	to see
avant d'avoir vu	before seeing (*lit:* having seen)
concret(-ète)	concrete
il se peut (que)	it's possible (that)
des frais (*m.*)	expenses
occasionné	incurred
en mesure de	capable of
soit dit entre nous	between you and me
il faut voir	we shall have to see
déjà	already
quelque chose	something
c'est déjà quelque chose	that's something

EXERCISE 5: Discussing delays

This practice enables you to check on many useful expressions used to discuss time spans, deadlines, etc. Remember to try and fit in some pronunciation practice if you can. In this exercise, for instance, you could work on the following words:
six (the **x** is not pronounced when **six** is followed by another word starting with a consonant. Before a vowel, **six** is pronounced **siz.**);
optimiste, transporter, encore, sorte, négociations: sound **o**; ess*a*yer, j*ui*n, h*ui*t.

LANGUAGE NOTES

32   **Faites en sorte qu'il soit là-bas ...**
Subjunctive after **en sorte que.**

VOCABULARY

le délai	time required for delivery
la date limite	deadline
utile	useful
fabriquer	to make, produce
essayer	to test
compter	to allow (time)
prudent	wise
sans faute	without fail
(faire) de mon mieux	(to do) my best
(bien) se passer	to go (well)
optimiste	optimistic

SCENE 6: Geneva – in a car and the office

After the meeting with Mohamed, Catherine, Pierre and Jean-Pierre discuss their chances of obtaining the contract. Catherine is optimistic and thinks that, if it depends only on Mohamed, they are likely to get it. Pierre tries to get Catherine to have dinner with him, but she asks him to forget about it; she thinks it is useless for them to go out together, as he will probably be going to Mexico anyway. Pierre wishes to know if Alain Tanner has also got something to do with her attitude, and Catherine admits that he has. In fact Tanner phones in the middle of their conversation, and Catherine chooses to take the call in her office. That does it for Pierre, who decides then and there to go to Mexico. Catherine tries to resume their conversation when she comes back from her office, but Pierre cuts her short, and Catherine is annoyed. She then goes off with Jean-Pierre to start work on the Egyptian project.

LANGUAGE NOTES

18 **N'en parlons plus**
With a negative Imperative, **en** comes between **ne** and the verb: *Let's not talk about it any more.* Same word order with y: **N'y pensons plus, N'y allons pas,** etc.

27 **C'aurait été bien que vous restiez ...**
Note the use of the Subjunctive here, after **c'aurait été bien que.**

34 **J'ai trouvé que ça avait bien marché**
The sequence of tenses in French is different from the English one: when the first verb is in the Perfect or Imperfect tense, the second one is in the Pluperfect.

83 **... l'homme le plus agaçant que je connaisse**
Another construction with a verb in the Subjunctive:
le (la, les) plus + adjective + **que** + verb in Subjunctive.

VOCABULARY

un avis	opinion
à votre avis	in your opinion
partir	to leave
en partant	when he left
ça ira	everything will be OK
mener	to take, lead
ça ne nous mènerait nulle part	that wouldn't get us anywhere
réfléchir	to think
vous avez réfléchi?	have you thought about it?
passer	to put (a call) through
vous pouvez me le passer?	can you put it through (to me)
un appel	phone call
en ligne	on the line
ça y est	that's that
à quel sujet	about what?
agaçant	aggravating
bien	much, far
fier	proud
un ennui	a problem
s'attirer des ennuis	to bring problems on oneself

Cassette 4   Side 2
I'd better be going

SCENE 1: The Geneva office

Pierre is dictating letters to his secretary. He begins by dictating a letter for a Patrick Loriot in Mexico, telling him that he has decided to stay in Geneva. He then changes his mind and decides to dictate instead a letter addressed to a Mr. G. Floret in Paris, in which he states that, contrary to what he had said at first, he has now made up his mind to stay in Geneva. He also asks Mr. Floret if he could possibly intervene in his favor.

LANGUAGE NOTES

7   **Après avoir longuement réfléchi**
The Past Infinitive is used after **après:** here the sentence means, literally: *After having thought for a long time.* Compare with the English equivalent: *After thinking for a long time.*

18   **Peut-être vous serait-il possible de m'aider**
This choice of word order, with **peut-être** placed at the beginning of the sentence, and the inversion of verb and subject, is a fairly formal one.

21   **En vous remerciant d'avance …**
Another instance here of the use of **en** followed by the Present Participle: *Thanking you …*

VOCABULARY

une virgule	comma
à la ligne	new paragraph
un point	period
il se trouve (que)	it turns out, happens (that)
demeurer	to stay
user de ses bons offices	to use one's good offices
un point d'interrogation	question mark
je vous prie etc.	Yours etc.

EXERCISE 1: Letter-writing

This practice is doubly useful: it actually tells you how to lay out a letter in French, and while doing so it also teaches you the vocabulary relating to the subject.

LANGUAGE NOTES

38 **De façon amicale**
Note the use of **de,** to mean *in* (*a friendly way*).
One could also have said **de manière amicale.**

VOCABULARY

disposer (une lettre)	to lay out (a letter)
en haut	at the top
à droite	on the right
un lieu	location, place
à gauche	on the left
plus bas	lower
un expéditeur (*m.*)	sender
une ligne plus bas	one line down from
au milieu	in the middle
un destinataire	recipient
rédiger (une lettre)	to write (a letter)
terminer (une lettre)	to end, sign off (a letter)
une façon	way
amical, amicale (*m.f.*)	friendly
bien amicalement	Yours (letter)
formel/protocolaire	formal
sincère	sincere, truthful
respectueux	respectful
distingué	refined, distinguished
Veuillez agréer, Monsieur, mes sincères salutations	Yours sincerely
Je vous prie d'agréer, Monsieur, l'expression de mes sentiments respectueux/distingués	Yours faithfully

SCENE 2: The Geneva office

Françoise wants to speak to Pierre about the first meeting of the committee, which is due to take place on the third of the month. The man who was supposed to come from Paris to attend will be a day late. Pierre gets very cross and wants to know who Françoise talked to, whether it was to the right person. Françoise does not know who was on the phone with the message. Pierre then asks her to call Paris and talk to Duquesne in person, nobody else, and to make it clear that they want the senior engineer for the meeting on the third.

LANGUAGE NOTES

8 **C'est bien celle-là**
You have seen **bien** used in a question, to elicit confirmation. Here, its use is to give confirmation. In English, one would just stress the verb in the sentence: *Yes it IS that one.*

30 **Ne parlez à personne d'autre**
Another instance of this construction with **quelque chose/ rien/personne** + **de/d'** + adjective.

36 **Le moindre problème**
You know the superlative of superiority: **le/la/les plus ...**; this is the superlative of inferiority: **le/la/les moindre(s):** *the least, the smallest.*

VOCABULARY

avoir lieu	to take place
au point	OK, ready
manquer	to be missing
(il) manque	(he's) missing
se libérer	to be free (for a meeting)
en personne	in person
personne d'autre	nobody else
le moindre	the slightest

EXERCISE 2: Giving orders

Another exercise on direct/indirect speech, which practises both the Infinitive and Imperative forms of verbs.

LANGUAGE NOTES

... facile d'organiser/La manière de donner/Dites-lui de se calmer .../... et de ne pas s'inquiéter
Note the frequency with which the preposition **de** is used: after an adjective, after a noun, after the verb **dire**. In the negative, the word order is **... de + ne pas +** Infinitive.

25 **... sur le bouton de gauche**
Again, **de** is used, here to indicate a position. Similarly, one would say: **le bouton de droite** *(on the right)*.

VOCABULARY

décidément	there's no doubt about it, indeed
donner des ordres	to give orders
au secours!	help!
une cravate	tie
pris, prise (*m.f.*)	caught
une photocopieuse	photocopier
se calmer	to calm down
s'inquiéter	to worry
un type (de machine)	kind, type (of machine)
tirer	to pull
dessus	on it
couper	to switch off
le courant	power, electricity
un couvercle	top, cover
un rouleau	roller
laisser	to drop, to let fall
dégagé	free
remettre le courant	to switch on (again)
à l'avenir	in future

SCENE 3: The Geneva office

At the beginning of the scene Françoise comes to see
Pierre to give him M. Duquesne's reply about the meeting
on the third. He will come. Pierre thanks Françoise for
making the phone call and congratulates her for dealing
efficiently with Duquesne. Françoise then asks him
whether he really intends to leave for Mexico. Pierre
confirms that he does, and Françoise wants to know why he
does not look happier about it, and why he does not talk
to Catherine if he has, as it seems, changed his mind and
no longer wants to go. At this point, Catherine comes in;
she wants to talk to Pierre. Pierre tells her he wanted to
speak to her too, and – as Françoise leaves – proceeds to
ask her how things stand between Tanner and her.
Apparently everything is finished, and on hearing this
Pierre announces that he has now decided to stay in
Geneva. Catherine approves of the idea, and it is very
clear that she would love Pierre to stay. However, it
transpires that she has already taken steps to replace him,
and on hearing who is due to take his job, we are not
altogether surprised that Pierre does not readily agree ...

LANGUAGE NOTES

8 **Merci de vous en être occupée**
The Past Infinitive is used in French when the action
referred to happened in the Past.

26 **... elle préférerait que vous restiez**
Subjunctive after **préférer que.**

41 **Avant qu'il ne soit trop tard**
Notice the Subjunctive after **avant que,** and the use of **ne,**
which is not a real negation. It is just automatically used in
connection with the Subjunctive after certain set phrases
or verbs.

61 **Vous voulez savoir où en sont les choses entre Alain et moi?**
Note this way of saying ... *where things stand,* using **en.**
Similarly, if one wants to know where someone is in
something they are doing, one will ask: **Où en es-tu?/Où
en êtes-vous?**

66 **... je lui ai dit que tout était fini**
An example of the sequence of tenses in French: first verb
in the Perfect tense, second verb in the Imperfect.

99 **J'ai entendu dire que vous n'aviez pas été très poli avec lui**
Again, the second verb is in the Pluperfect tense when the
first one is in the Perfect in French — when the
second action was accomplished before the first one.

VOCABULARY

ferme	firm
entendre dire	to hear (it said)
j'ai entendu dire (que)	I hear (that)
j'en ai l'intention	I intend to
ça ne me regarde pas	it's none of my business
quinze jours	two weeks
changer d'avis	to change one's mind
où en sont les choses	how things stand
je n'y verrais pas d'inconvénient	that would suit me
mettre (quelqu'un) au courant	to show (someone) the ropes
un remplaçant	replacement
le métier	job
arranger (quelque chose)	to settle, arrange (something)
un type	guy (*familiar*)
un type pareil	a guy like that
poli	polite
Il n'y a rien à faire!	No way, nothing doing

EXERCISE 3: Listening and understanding (2)

This is a listening and comprehension exercise. Listen to each part carefully and try to memorize the key words to sum up what you have just heard.

LANGUAGE NOTES

11   **... c'est là qu'elle en a entendu parler**
Again, note the contrast between the English way of stressing (*that's* where she heard about it) merely by using one's voice, and the French way, in which a different grammatical construction has to be used in order to stress a particular word or group of words.

15   **... quand il sera libre**
Note that in French **quand** can be followed by the Future tense. Compare with English: *when it's free.*

35   **visiter le sien**
Le sien (la sienne, les siens/les siennes) is the possessive pronoun meaning *his* or *hers,* referring to a masculine singular object, here **un appartement.**

VOCABULARY

s'entendre	to get along (with somebody)
un exercice d'écoute	listening exercise
destiné à	for (message, letter)
apparemment	apparently
à mi-temps	part-time
se loger	to live, to find somewhere to live
elle cherche à se loger	she's looking for somewhere to live
sauf	except
entendre parler (de quelque chose)	to hear about (something)
elle en a entendu parler	she's heard about it

SCENE 4: The Geneva office

Catherine introduces Melville and Pierre to each other ...
again, and leaves them after a few minutes. Pierre and
Melville both assure each other that neither bears a
grudge. Melville explains to Pierre that he just wants to
attend the first meeting, but that he does not want to
interfere in any way. Pierre asks Melville bluntly why he
has decided to change his job, and tries to persuade him
not to take up the post. But Melville is not inclined to
change his mind ...

LANGUAGE NOTES

19 **Mais je vous laisse entièrement faire ...**
Laisser + Infinitive means *to let (someone) do
(something)*.

58 **Vous changerez peut-être d'avis, quand vous aurez
réfléchi**
Sequence of tenses in the Future: when the first verb is in
the Future tense, the second verb is in the Future tense or
in the Future Perfect.

60 **Non, sûrement pas**
Note the non-verbal answer, with the negation **pas**:
certainly not.

VOCABULARY

laisser	to leave
je vous laisse	I'll leave you to it, I'm off
sans rancune?	no hard feelings?
pourtant	though
se faire une idée (de)	to get some idea (of something)
navré	very sorry
avoir l'air (d'un imbécile)	to look (like a fool)
un poste	post (job)
au contraire	on the contrary
une raison	reason

EXERCISE 4: Questions and answers

This exercise enables you to practise many typical questions and answers used in every day spoken French, and in particular the use of **si,** as a positive response to a negative question.

LANGUAGE NOTES

12 **Vous êtes déjà allé à Londres, non?**
Non is sometimes used in this way at the end of a sentence to mean *haven't you?/isn't he/she?/don't you/they?,* etc. Note the intonation in this type of sentence.

17 **Et les Etats-Unis, vous n'y allez pas cette année?**
Make a note of this construction, very common in French, with the name of the place in question at the beginning of the sentence, and referred to in the later part of the sentence with help of the pronoun **y.**

19 **Si, j'irai sans doute en automne**
Note that **en** is the preposition used with names of seasons, except for **printemps:**
> **en automne,**
> **en hiver,**
> **en été,**
but **au printemps.**

20 **Et vous n'emmènerez pas votre femme non plus?**
Non plus is used in conjunction with **ne ... pas** to mean *neither, not either.*

VOCABULARY

un séjour	(a) stay
si	yes (in contradiction)
emmener	to take (with one)
vous emmenez votre femme?	are you taking your wife with you?
vous n'emmènerez pas votre femme	you won't be taking your wife
réviser	to revise

SCENE 5: The Geneva office

Pierre and Melville are having a chat after the meeting. Melville is impressed by the engineers' professionalism. Pierre phones through to his office to check if there are any messages for him. Françoise reads out to him a letter from CIT in Mexico: apparently Pierre is exactly the person they need, and they don't even need to interview him. Pierre is somewhat puzzled, and wonders what happened to the letter he sent them. As the only thing he will have to do in order to get the Mexico job is to have a medical check-up, he asks Melville jokingly what one has to do if one wants to fail a medical test. Then Françoise reads him a telex. It comes from Pascale, who seems to have understood at long last that Pierre no longer wants her for his secretary. Predictably, this news cheers Pierre up considerably. Finally, Françoise tells him that she has found a letter in his desk. It would seem he forgot to post it ... Pierre understands why he has been offered the job, and tries to get used to the idea of going to Mexico ... In the end, he goes back to the meeting with Melville.

LANGUAGE NOTES

10 **J'en ai pour une minute, à peine**
Note this use of **en** again, with the verb **avoir.** The English equivalent of this sentence would be: *It won't take me a minute.*

12 **Oui, c'est elle-même**
Make a note of this phrase, which is how one answers one's name on the phone. If the person who answers is a man, then of course he will say: **(Oui) c'est lui-même.**

... vous faire savoir/je leur ai envoyé/il ne nous semble pas nécessaire/La seule condition ..., qui vous semblera ...
All indirect pronouns are placed before the verb, as are direct pronouns. A table in the Appendix at the back of this book tells you in what order they are placed in the sentence.

35   **... tellement de bien de vous qu'il ne nous semble pas
nécessaire ...**
This is another way of saying in French: *so much ... that ...*
One could also have said, using an expression which you
have met before: **...tant de bien de vous...**

62   **Cassez-vous une jambe ... ou un bras**
Note this way of saying *to break one's leg/arm:* the
reflexive verb is used, with the indefinite article **un/une,** or
the definite article **le/la/les.**

83   **Je vous le lis?**
Here the Present tense is used in the same way as in
English we say *Shall I ...?* The sentence means *Shall I read
it to you?*

90   **Vous auriez pu me le dire**
The verb **pouvoir** is in the Past Conditional tense. This
tense is formed with the auxiliary verb **avoir** or **être** in
the Present Conditional tense and the Past Participle of
the verb being conjugated (here: **pu,** from **pouvoir**).
You will find this tense listed in the Grammatical
Appendix at the back of the book.

108   **En rangeant votre bureau hier j'ai trouvé cette lettre**
While I was tidying up ...
En + Present Participle indicates simultaneity with
another action.

111   **Ce n'est pas étonnant qu'ils n'aient rien reçu**
Subjunctive after **Ce n'est pas étonnant que.**

125   **Vous ne croyez pas qu'on ferait mieux de ...?**
Make a note of this expression which is used very
frequently in French: *Don't you think we'd better ...?*

VOCABULARY

je vous en prie	please do
allez-y	go ahead
à l'appareil	(Pierre) here (on phone)
flûte!	damn!
des mauvaises nouvelles	bad news
pourtant	but
dans un sens	in a way
convaincu	convinced
accueillir	to welcome
dans l'attente (de)	I look forward (to)
échouer	to fail
une visite médicale	medical (test)
aveugle	blind
sourd	deaf
tomber malade	to fall ill
casser	to break
une jambe	a leg
un bras	an arm
enlever (un manteau)	to take off (a coat)
vouloir de (quelqu'un)	to want (anything to do with) somebody
se retrouver (dans)	to find one's way through, to make sense of
un somnifère	sleeping-pill(s)

EXERCISE 5: Insisting on things

We have come across numerous examples of these sentence patterns with **c'est** throughout the Course so far – now is your chance to use them yourself, in context, and to put them into practice. Pay attention to the intonation as well.

LANGUAGE NOTES

1 **... de plus en plus vite**
De plus en plus *(more and more)* is followed by an adjective or an adverb: **de plus en plus beau/grand/fatigué/ facilement/tard.** etc.

Vous savez faire cet exercice?/Je saurai un peu mieux utiliser ...
In order to indicate that one is *able to do something/knows how to do something,* one uses the verb **savoir** followed by a verb in the Infinitive.

VOCABULARY

une genre	(a) kind
philosophe	philosophical
une nouvelle	a piece of news

SCENE 6: Geneva airport

Catherine and Pierre are at the airport. It is time for Pierre to board the plane, and Catherine wishes him good luck in his new job. She says she hopes they will meet again, when his three-year contract is finished. Pierre for his part wishes Catherine good luck with the Egyptian contract and with Melville; when the hostess calls the passengers, he leaves Catherine to board the plane with the defiant words: Mexico, here I come!

LANGUAGE NOTES

6 **Les passagers ayant ...**
The Present Participle is used as an adjective here, to
accompany the noun.

10 **Il faut que j'y aille**
Subjunctive after **il faut que.**
In French **y** must be included in the sentence to complete
the verb.

11 **On se reverra**
The synonym of **Nous nous reverrons:** *We'll see each other
again.*

27 **J'espère que vous l'aurez**
In French the Future tense has got to be used here. In
English, one could say: *I hope you get it,* using the Present
tense.

42 **Les passagers qui ne seraient pas encore présentés ...**
The Conditional indicates a possibility, a situation which
might arise/have arisen: *Passengers who might not have
yet ...*

VOCABULARY

une porte	gate (airport)
à destination de	(leaving) for
l'embarquement	boarding
carte d'embarquement	boarding pass
se présenter	to check in (in an airport)
prier	to request (to beg)
immédiat	immediate
immédiatement	immediately
un passager	passenger

GRAMMATICAL APPENDICES

Grammatical Appendices

1 Articles

DEFINITE			INDEFINITE		
Singular	Plural		Singular	Plural	
Masculine le l' before vowel and mute **h**	les		Masculine un	des	
Feminine la l' before vowel	les		Feminine une	des	

DEFINITE ARTICLE + à AND de			

au (à + le):
à l' before
   vowel and
   mute h
	au patron
	à l'ami
	à l'homme
		du (de + le):
		de l' before
		   vowel and
		   mute h
			du patron
			de l'ami
			de l'homme

à la
à l' before
   vowel and
   mute h
	à la secrétaire
	à l'étudiante
	à l'horlogerie
		de la
		de l' before
		   vowel and
		   mute h
			de la secrétaire
			de l'étudiante
			de l'horlogerie

aux (à + les)	**aux patrons** **aux amis** **aux hommes** **aux femmes** **aux horloges**	**des**	**des patrons** **des amis** **des hommes** **des femmes** **des horloges**

Use of the articles

USE OF THE DEFINITE ARTICLE .
1 Before abstract and general nouns: **elle a trouvé le bonheur.**
2 Before the name of a language: **elle étudie le français.**
3 Before titles of ranks or professions: **le général de Gaulle,
   le docteur Courtin.**
4 Before names of countries, continents, mountains, etc:
   la France est un beau pays, je connais le Mont Blanc.

5 Before parts of the body (where English would use a possessive adjective): **elle a les cheveux noirs, il se lave les mains, elles se brossent les dents.**

OMISSION OF THE INDEFINITE ARTICLE

1 Before names of professions and nationalities not qualified by an adjective: **il est français, Pierre est professeur, mon cousin est ingénieur.**
But notice: **Delphine est une excellente pianiste.**
2 With the exclamatory **quel: quel beau film! quelles jolies robes!**
3 With **cent** and **mille: il y a mille élèves dans son école.**

The partitive article: du, de la, des

This article is used where in English *some* or *any*, or *no/not any,* would be used. It refers to a part, a portion, an indefinite quantity of something.

SINGULAR		PLURAL
Masculine	Feminine	
du:	**de la:**	**des**
du vin	**de la patience**	
du pain	**de la chance**	
de l' before vowel or mute h:	**de l'** before vowel or mute h:	**des**
de l'argent	**de l'eau**	
de l'humour	**de l'huile**	

After a negation such as **pas** and **jamais, un, une, des** and **du, de, la, des** become **de.** Thus:

J'ai un livre.		**Je n'ai pas de cassette.**
J'ai une cassette.	become	**Je n'ai pas de cassette.**
J'ai des bureaux.		**Je n'ai pas de bureau.**
J'ai du pain.		**Je n'ai pas de pain.**
J'ai de la chance.	become	**Je n'ai pas de chance.**
J'ai des amis.		**Je n'ai pas d'amis.**

2   Adjectives and Adverbs

Every adjective must be made to agree in gender and number with the noun or pronoun which it modifies, which it refers to.

Formation of the feminine

Type of adjective	Masculine	Feminine
A Regular	**petit, grand**	+ e: **petite, grande**
B Ending in -e	**aimable, rouge**	same: **aimable, rouge**
C Ending in -f	**actif, neuf**	-ve: **active, neuve**
D Ending in -er	**cher, premier**	-ère: **chère, première**
E Ending in -eux, and some in -eur	**heureux, flatteur**	-euse: **heureuse, flatteuse**

EXCEPTIONS

vieux	**vieille**	*old*
majeur	**majeure**	*major, of age*
mineur	**mineure**	*minor, underage*
meilleur	**meilleure**	*better*
extérieur	**extérieure**	*exterior, outer*

You will also come across a number of common adjectives which have an irregular feminine, such as **ancien/ancienne, doux/douce, fou/folle, beau/belle,** etc.

The adjectives **beau, vieux, nouveau** each have a special form in the masculine singular when they are placed before a noun beginning with a vowel or a mute **h:**

le beau tableau	but	**le bel été, le bel arbre**
le beau bureau		**le bel homme, le bel hôtel**
le vieux livre	but	**le vieil ami, le vieil arbre**
le vieux disque		**le vieil homme, le vieil hôtel**
le nouveau directeur	but	**le nouvel ami**
le nouveau patron		**le nouvel hôtel**

Plural of adjectives

FEMININE ADJECTIVES
Since all feminine adjectives end in **-e,** they all form the
plural by adding an **-s** to the singular:

la jolie maison	**les jolies maisons**
une femme heureuse	**des femmes heureuses,** etc.

MASCULINE ADJECTIVES

Type of adjective	Singular	Plural
A Regular	**le restaurant cher** **le tapis bleu**	**- + s les restaurants** **chers** **les tapis bleus**
B Ending in -s or **-x**	**l'homme heureux** **le gros chien**	same **les hommes** **heureux** **les gros chiens**
C Ending in **-eau**	**le beau pays**	**- + x les beaux pays**
D Ending in **-al**	**le point principal**	**-aux les points** **principaux**

Position of adjectives

Usually, adjectives are placed after the noun which they
describe:

> **la maison blanche, le pied droit,**
> **une chanteuse célèbre, un repas délicieux**

However, the following common adjectives are nearly
always placed before the noun:

bon	**vilain**	**gros**
mauvais	**jeune**	**petit**
beau	**vieux**	**long**
joli	**grand**	**court**

Comparative and superlative forms of the adjective

COMPARATIVES

1 Superiority: **plus ... que**   **Delphine est plus jolie qu'Odile**
2 Equality: **aussi ... que**   **Delphine est aussi jolie qu'Odile**
3 Inferiority: **moins ... que**   **Delphine est moins jolie qu'Odile**

SUPERLATIVES

The superlative form of the adjective is used when three or more things are being compared. It is obtained by putting the definite article or a possessive adjective before the comparative.

1 Adjectives placed before the noun   **la plus grosse voiture**
     mon plus vieil ami
2 Adjectives placed after the noun   **l'élève le plus intelligent**
     mon amie la plus fidèle
3 After a superlative, the English *in* is rendered as **de**   **la plus belle ville de France**
     l'homme le plus riche du monde

IRREGULAR ADJECTIVES

All forms of these irregular adjectives usually precede the noun.

Adjective	Comparative	Superlative
bon/bonne	**meilleur/meilleure meilleurs/meilleures**	**le meilleur/les meilleurs la meilleure/les meilleures**
mauvais/ mauvaise	**pire(s) plus mauvais/ mauvaise(s)**	**le pire/la pire/les pires le plus mauvais la plus mauvaise les plus mauvais(es)**
petit/petite	**moindre(s) plus petit/plus petite/ plus petits/plus petites**	**le moindre/la moindre les moindres le plus petit/la plus petite les plus petits/ les plus petites**

Comparative and superlative of adverbs

1 Comparison of adverbs is also expressed through the use of
plus ... que, aussi ... que, moins ... que. For example:
Pierre marche plus vite/aussi vite/moins vite que moi.
2 The superlative is formed by adding **le plus** in front of the
adverb: **Eric parle le plus fort.**

IRREGULAR COMPARATIVES AND SUPERLATIVES

bien	**mieux**	**le mieux**
mal	**pis**	**le pis**
beaucoup	**plus**	**le plus**
peu	**moins**	**le moins**

3 Possessives

Adjectives

Singular		Plural
Masculine	Feminine	
mon	ma	mes
ton	ta	tes
son	sa	ses
notre	notre	nos
votre	votre	vos
leur	leur	leurs

Possessive adjectives agree in French with the thing possessed. This is particularly relevant for an English-speaking student of the language since in English in the third person singular *his* and *her* agree with the possessor, not the thing (or person!) possessed as in French.

Mon, ton and **son** are used instead of **ma, ta** and **sa,** respectively, when the feminine noun which follows begins with a vowel or a mute **h.** This is done for euphonic reasons: **Une amie, une histoire: Mon amie, mon histoire.**

Pronouns

These are the same in gender and number as the thing (or person) possessed. Note the use of the definite article with these pronouns:

Singular		Plural	
Masculine	Feminine	Masculine	Feminine
le mien	la mienne	les miens	les miennes
le tien	la tienne	les tiens	les tiennes
le sien	la sienne	les siens	les siennes
le nôtre	la nôtre	les nôtres	les nôtres
le vôtre	la vôtre	les vôtres	les vôtres
le leur	la leur	les leurs	les leurs

4 Demonstratives

Adjectives

Singular		Plural	
Masculine	Feminine	Masculine	Feminine

ce
cet (before
    vowel and
    mute **h**)
ce ... ci
ce ... là
	cette
	
	cette ... ci
	cette ... là
		ces
		
		ces ... ci
		ces ... là
			ces
			
			ces ... ci
			ces ... là

Ce, cet, cette, ces can mean both *this/that (these/those)*.
Ci and **là** are used to differentiate between two groups of
people or things, one near and one far:
>   **ces livres-ci sont à moi, ces livres-là sont à lui.**
Cet is used before nouns beginning with a vowel or a mute **h**:
>   **cet arbre, cet enfant, cet élève, cet homme.**

Pronouns

Singular		Plural	
Masculine	Feminine	Masculine	Feminine
celui **celui-ci** **celui-là**	**celle** **celle-ci** **celle-là**	**ceux** **ceux-ci** **ceux-là**	**celles** **celles-ci** **celles-là**

5   Interrogatives

Adjectives

These adjectives correspond to both *which?* and *what?*
and refer to both persons and things.

Singular		Plural	
Masculine	Feminine	Masculine	Feminine
quel?	quelle?	quels?	quelles?

Pronouns

FOR PERSONS

1 Subject   **Qui est responsable?**
                       Qui est-ce qui est responsable?

2 Object   **Qui cherchez-vous?**
                       Qui est-ce que vous cherchez?

3 With prepositions **Avec qui allez-vous a Paris?**
                       A qui parliez-vous?

FOR THINGS

1 Subject   **Qu'est-ce qui est arrivé?**

2 Object   **Que voulez-vous?**
                       Qu'est-ce que vous voulez?

3 With prepositions **De quoi parlez-vous?**

PRONOUNS INDICATING *WHICH ONE?/WHICH ONES?*

Singular		Plural	
Masculine	Feminine	Masculine	Feminine
lequel	laquelle	lesquels	lesquelles
auquel	à laquelle	auxquels	auxquelles
duquel	de laquelle	desquels	desquelles
avec lequel	avec laquelle	avec lesquels	avec lesquelles, etc.

6   Object pronouns

Direct object pronouns

me	nous
te	vous
le/la	les

For instance:

Elle me voit	**Nous te croyons**
Ils la regardent	**Vous le savez** etc.

In sentences where the verb is in the affirmative Imperative, **moi** is used as direct object pronoun instead if **me:**

Regardez-moi   **Aide-moi**   etc.

Indirect object pronouns

me	nous
te	vous
lui	leur

For example:

Elle lui parle	**Nous leur avons téléphoné**
Vous me donnez un livre	**Tu lui as écrit** etc.

In affirmative Imperative sentences, **moi** is used instead of **me** as indirect pronoun:

Vous me donnez un livre	but	**Donnez-moi un livre**
Tu me téléphones	but	**Téléphone-moi** etc.

Reflexive pronouns

me	nous
te	vous
se	se

In affirmative Imperative sentences, **toi** is used instead of **te:**

Tu te dépêches	but	**Dépêche-toi**
Tu t'amuses	but	**Amuse-toi** etc.

Y and EN

Y – USE AND MEANING

1 **Y** replaces a preposition, such as **à,** plus a place mentioned:

Il est au bureau?	**Oui, il y est.**
Tu vas à Paris?	**Oui, j'y vais demain.**

2 **Y** replaces **à,** plus an idea or thing mentioned:

Tu penses à ton pays?	**Oui, j'y pense souvent.**
Elle a répondu à ta lettre?	**Oui, elle y a répondu.**

En – USE AND MEANING

1 **En** replaces **de,** plus a place mentioned:

Vous venez de Londres?	**Oui, j'en viens.**
Vous sortez du théâtre?	**Oui, j'en sors.**

2 **En** replaces **de,** plus an idea or a thing mentioned:

Vous parlez du film?	**Oui, nous en parlons.**
Tu te souviens de ces vacances?	**Oui, je m'en souviens.**

3 **En** has the meaning of *some, any* or *none:*

Tu as de l'argent?	**Oui, j'en ai.**
Vous avez pris du café?	**Oui, j'en ai pris.**

4 **En,** in this sense, must always be expressed:

Il a des frères et sœurs?	**Oui, il en a cinq.**
Faites trois exercises.	**Faites-en trois.**

POSITION OF PRONOUNS

In all sentences except sentences in which the verb is in the affirmative Imperative:

	me					
	te	le	lui			
Subject (+ **ne**) +	se	la	leur	y	en	+ verb
	nous	les				
	vous					

7 Relative pronouns

Qui, que, lequel, dont

	PERSONS	THINGS
Subject	**qui**	**qui**
Object	**que**	**que**
With prepositions	**qui** or **lequel lesquels laquelle lesquelles**	**lequel lesquels laquelle lesquelles**
With **de**	**dont**	**dont**

Dont is the French equivalent of *whose* and *of whom*
in English, and is used as a replacement of **de** + **qui/que**,
with verbs like **parler** which take the preposition **de**.
For example:
> **Voilà l'amie dont je t'ai parlé.**
> **J'ai trouvé le livre dont tu m'avais donné le titre.**

Ce qui, ce que, quoi

The three pronouns above correspond to the English pronoun
what. **Ce qui** and **ce que**, are used instead of **qu'est-ce
qui** and **qu'est-ce que** in reported speech:

Direct speech	Reported speech
Qu'est-ce qui est arrivé? **Qu'est-ce qu'il y a?**	**Dis-moi ce qui est arrivé.** **Je me demande ce qu'il y a.**
Qu'est-ce que vous voulez?	**Je ne sais pas ce que vous voulez.**
Qu'est-ce que tu fais?	**Explique-moi ce que tu fais.**

8 Position of adverbs

Adverbs, words such as **souvent, quelquefois, déjà, demain, bientôt** can be placed in different parts of the sentence, and sometimes the same adverb can be positioned both at the beginning or the end of the sentence. It is therefore practically impossible to give rigid rules as to the position of adverbs, but the following guidelines should prove useful:

1 Usually, the adverb is placed after the verb:
  Il vient souvent nous voir.
  Je t'écrirai bientôt.

2 As a rule, it comes before an adjective or another adverb:
  Il est bien gentil.
  Il téléphone presque toujours le matin.

3 It usually comes before the Infinitive and the Past Participle:
  Je l'avais déjà remarqué.
  Ils vont surtout parler des problèmes financiers.

4 Adverbial phrases, on account of their greater length, are usually placed at the end of the sentence:
  Il est passé nous voir tout à l'heure.
  J'espère les revoir dans peu de temps.

9 Negation

Some negative expressions:

ne ... pas	*not*	**Elle n'a pas de chance.**
ne ... plus	*no more, no longer*	**Je n'ai plus d'argent.**
ne ... jamais	*never*	**Il ne va jamais la voir.**
ne ... personne	*no one*	**Je ne connais personne.**
ne ... rien	*nothing*	**Elle ne comprend rien.**
ne ... que	*nothing but, only*	**Il n'a qu'une sœur.**
ne ... ni ... ni	*neither ... nor*	**Il n'a ni argent ni amis.**

Personne and **rien** can also be placed at the beginning of the sentence, as subjects of the verb. In that case they are immediately followed by **ne,** and **pas** is omitted:

  Personne n'est venu. **Rien ne marche.**
  Personne n'est d'accord. **Rien ne me plaît.**

10 Numerals, dates and times

Cardinal numbers

1	un, une	*15*	quinze	*41*	quarante et un
2	deux	*16*	seize	*50*	cinquante
3	trois	*17*	dix-sept	*51*	cinquante et un
4	quatre	*18*	dix-huit	*60*	soixante
5	cinq	*19*	dix-neuf	*61*	soixante et un
6	six	*20*	vingt	*70*	soixante-dix
7	sept	*21*	vingt et un	*71*	soixante et onze
8	huit	*22*	vingt-deux	*72*	soixante-douze
9	neuf	*23*	vingt-trois	*75*	soixante-quinze
10	dix	*30*	trente	*76*	soixante-seize
11	onze	*31*	trente et un	*79*	soixante-dix-neuf
12	douze	*32*	trente-deux	*80*	quatre-vingts
13	treize	*40*	quarante	*81*	quatre-vingt-un
14	quatorze				

82	quatre-vingt-deux	*200*	deux cents
90	quatre-vingt-dix	*201*	deux cent un
91	quatre-vingt-onze	*900*	neuf cents
99	quatre-vingt-dix-neuf	*1 000*	mille
100	cent	*1 001*	mille un
101	cent un	*1 900*	mille neuf cents
102	cent deux	*2 000*	deux mille
121	cent vingt et un	*900 000*	neuf cent mille
		1 000 000	un million

Ordinal numbers

1st	premier, première	*8th*	huitième
2d	deuxième, second(e)	*9th*	neuvième
3d	troisième	*10th*	dixième
4th	quatrième	*11th*	onzième
5th	cinquième	*21st*	vingt et unième
6th	sixième	*100th*	centième
7th	septième	*1 000th*	millième
		last	dernier, dernière

Expression of dates

In expressing dates, **le premier** is used for the first day of the month, while the cardinal numbers are used for all the other days. The word *on* or *of,* used when giving dates in English, does not have an equivalent in French:

Quel jour sommes-nous
Le combien sommes-nous   **aujourd'hui?**   *What is today's*
Le combien est-ce   *date?*

> **Aujourd'hui c'est/nous sommes**
>   **le premier janvier**   **le quatre juillet**
>   **le seize juin**   **le trente et un août**

In dates, one thousand is spelled **mil** (rather than **mille**):

1936	**mil neuf cent trente-six** or
	dix-neuf cent trente-six
1789	**mil sept cent quatre-vingt-neuf** or
	dix-neuf cent quatre-vingt-neuf
1900	**mil neuf cents**
July 14, 1789	**le quatorze juillet mil sept cent**
	quatre-vingt-neuf

Also note this way of referring to decades:
     les années quatre-vingts   *the eighties*

Days of the week, seasons and months

All these words are masculine in French and are not capitalized:

Days				**Seasons**	
lundi	*Monday*	**vendredi**	*Friday*	**au printemps**	*in Spring*
mardi	*Tuesday*	**samedi**	*Saturday*	**en été**	*in Summer*
mercredi	*Wednesday*	**dimanche**	*Sunday*	**en automne**	*in Autumn*
jeudi	*Thursday*			**en hiver**	*in Winter*

Months			
janvier	*January*	**juillet**	*July*
février	*February*	**août**	*August*
mars	*March*	**septembre**	*September*
avril	*April*	**octobre**	*October*
mai	*May*	**novembre**	*November*
juin	*June*	**décembre**	*December*

A FEW COMMON EXPRESSIONS OF TIME

lundi dernier	*last Monday*
mardi prochain	*next Tuesday*
aujourd'hui	*today*
demain	*tomorrow*
hier	*yesterday*
après-demain	*the day after tomorrow*
avant-hier	*the day before yesterday*
cette semaine	*this week*
la semaine prochaine	*next week*
la semaine dernière	*last week*
ce mois-ci	*this month*
le mois prochain	*next month*
le mois dernier	*last month*
quinze jours	*two weeks*
cette année	*this year*
l'année prochaine	*next year*
l'année dernière	*last year*
tous les ans	*every year*
toute l'année	*all year*
tous les jours	*every day*
toutes les semaines	*every week*
tous les mois	*every month*
tous les ans	*every year*
tous les quinze jours	*every two weeks*
huit jours	*a week*
il y a huit jours	*a week ago*
dans huit jours	*in a week's time*
en huit jours	*within a week*
tous les deux jours	*every two days*
toutes les trois semaines	*every three weeks*
tous les six mois	*every six months*
tous les deux ans	*every two years*

11 Regular verbs

Group 1: Infinitive ending in -er
Infinitive: **donner** Present Participle: **donnant** Past Participle: **donné**

Present	Imperfect	Future
je donne	je donnais	je donnerai
tu donnes	tu donnais	tu donneras
il	il	il
elle donne	elle donnait	elle donnera
nous donnons	nous donnions	nous donnerons
vous donnez	vous donniez	vous donnerez
ils	ils	ils
elles donnent	elles donnaient	elles donneront

Future Perfect	Present Perfect	Pluperfect
j'aurai donné	j'ai donné	j'avais donné
tu auras donné	tu as donné	tu avais donné
il	il	il
elle aura donné	elle a donné	elle avait donné
nous aurons donné	nous avons donné	nous avions donné
vous aurez donné	vous avez donné	vous aviez donné
ils	ils	ils
elles auront donné	elles ont donné	elles avaient donné

Conditional	Past Conditional	Subjunctive (Present)
je donnerais	j'aurais donné	que je donne
tu donnerais	tu aurais donné	que tu donnes
il	il	qu'il
elle donnerait	elle aurait donné	qu'elle donne
nous donnerions	nous aurions donné	que nous donnions
vous donneriez	vous auriez donné	que vous donniez
ils	ils	qu'ils
elles donneraient	elles auraient donné	qu'elles donnent

Imperative: **donne   donnons   donnez**

Group 2: Infinitive ending in -ir

Infinitive: **finir**   Present Participle: **finissant**   Past Participle: **fini**

Present	Imperfect	Future
je finis	je finissais	je finirai
tu finis	tu finissais	tu finiras
il elle finit	il elle finissait	il elle finira
nous finissons	nous finissions	nous finirons
vous finissez	vous finissiez	vous finirez
ils elles finissent	ils elles finissaient	ils elles finiront

Future Perfect	Present Perfect	Pluperfect
j'aurai fini	j'ai fini	j'avais fini
tu auras fini	tu as fini	tu avais fini
il elle aura fini	il elle a fini	il elle avait fini
nous aurons fini	nous avons fini	nous avions fini
vous aurez fini	vous avez fini	vous aviez fini
ils elles auront fini	ils elles ont fini	ils elles avaient fini

Conditional	Past Conditional	Subjunctive
je finirais	j'aurais fini	que je finisse
tu finirais	tu aurais fini	que tu finisses
il elle finirait	il elle aurait fini	qu'il qu'elle finisse
nous finirions	nous aurions fini	que nous finissions
vous finiriez	vous auriez fini	que vous finissiez
ils elles finiraient	ils elles auraient fini	qu'ils qu'elles finissent

Imperative: **finis**   **finissons**   **finissez**

Group 3: Infinitive ending in -re

Infinitive: **vendre** Present Participle: **vendant** Past Participle **vendu**

Present	Imperfect	Future
je vends	je vendais	je vendrai
tu vends	tu vendais	tu vendras
il	il	il
elle vend	elle vendait	elle vendra
nous vendons	nous vendions	nous vendrons
vous vendez	vous vendiez	vous vendrez
ils	ils	ils
elles vendent	elles vendaient	elles vendront

Future Perfect	Present Perfect	Pluperfect
j'aurai vendu	j'ai vendu	j'avais vendu
tu auras vendu	tu as vendu	tu avais vendu
il	il	il
elle aura vendu	elle a vendu	elle avait vendu
nous aurons vendu	nous avons vendu	nous avions vendu
vous aurez vendu	vous avez vendu	vous aviez vendu
ils	ils	ils
elles auront vendu	elles ont vendu	elles avaient vendu

Conditional	Past Conditional	Subjunctive
je vendrais	j'aurais vendu	que je vende
tu vendrais	tu aurais vendu	que tu vendes
il	il	qu'il
elle vendrait	elle aurait vendu	qu'elle vende
nous vendrions	nous aurions vendu	que nous vendions
vous vendriez	vous auriez vendu	que vous vendiez
ils	ils auraient	qu'ils
elles vendraient	elles vendu	qu'elles vendent

Imperative: **vends**   **vendons**   **vendez**

Orthographic changes in regular verbs

Some verbs, regular in all other respects, undergo slight changes in spelling in certain persons and tenses. These changes, which affect only one letter in the word, are rendered necessary by the rules of pronunciation.

1 Verbs in **-ger**: In order to keep the soft sound of the **g**, an additional **e** must be inserted before endings which begin with **a** or **o**. For example, **manger**:

mangeant	**je mangeais**	**il mangeait**
nous mangeons	**tu mangeais**	**ils mangeaient**

2 Verbs in **-cer**: In order to keep the soft sound of the **c**, it must be change to **ç** before endings which begin with **a** or **o**. This occurs in the same places in which the **-ger** verbs require an **e**. For example, **commencer**:

commençant	**je commençais**	**il commençait**
nous commençons	**tu commençais**	**ils commençaient**

3 Verbs containing a mute **e** in their stem (= the part of the verb which does not change) such as **acheter, mener, promener, lever** require the grave accent (`) on that vowel when the next syllable also contains a mute **e**. This is because it would be too difficult to pronounce two successive syllables containing a mute **e**. For example, **acheter**:

j'achète	**que j'achète**	**j'achèterai**	**j'achèterais**
tu achètes	**que tu achètes**	**tu achèteras**	**tu achèterais**
il achète	**qu'il achète**	**il achètera**	**il achèterait**
ils achètent	**qu'ils achètent**	**nous achèterons**	**nous achèterions**
		vous achèterez	**vous achèteriez**
		ils achèteront	**ils achèteraient**

4 In verbs like **préférer, répéter**, the **é** changes to **è** before a mute **e** in the simple Present tense and the Present Subjunctive only. For example, **préférer**:

je préfère	**que je préfère**
tu préfères	**que tu préfères**
il préfère	**qu'il préfère**
ils préfèrent	**qu'ils préfèrent**

5 **Verbs in -yer** change the **y** to **i** before a mute **e.** For example, **nettoyer:**

Present	Subjunctive
je nettoie	**que je nettoie**
tu nettoies	**que tu nettoies**
il nettoie	**qu'il nettoie**
nous nettoyons	**que nous nettoyions**
vous nettoyez	**que vous nettoyiez**
ils nettoient	**qu'ils nettoient**

Future	Conditional
je nettoierai	**je nettoierais**
tu nettoieras	**tu nettoierais**
il nettoiera	**il nettoierait**
nous nettoierons	**nous nettoierions**
vous nettoierez	**vous nettoieriez**
ils nettoieront	**ils nettoieraient**

6 Verbs ending in **-ayer** may either retain the **y** before a mute **e,** or change to **i.** For example, **payer:**
Present   **je paye** or **je paie**
Future   **je payerai** or **je paierai,** etc.

7 Most verbs in **-eler** and **-eter** double the **l** or **t** before a mute **e** instead of taking the grave accent. The most common examples are **appeler** and **jeter:**

Present		Subjunctive	
j'appelle	**nous appelons**	**que j'appelle**	**que nous appelions**
tu appelles	**vous appelez**	**que tu appelles**	**que vous appeliez**
il appelle	**ils appellent**	**qu'il appelle**	**qu'ils appellent**

Future		Conditional	
j'appellerai	**nous appellerons**	**j'appellerais**	**nous appellerions**
tu appelleras	**vous appellerez**	**tu appellerais**	**vous appelleriez**
il appellera	**ils appelleront**	**il appellerait**	**ils appelleraient**

Similarly, with **jeter:**
Present   **je jette, tu jettes,** etc.
Future   **je jetterai, tu jetteras,** etc.

12   Regular verbs in the course

abandonner	1	choisir	2	développer	1
abattre	3	choquer	1	deviner	1
abimer	1	classer	1	diner	1
absorber	1	clignoter	1	diriger	1
accepter	1	collaborer	1	discuter	1
accompagner	1	coller	1	disposer de	1
accorder	1	commander	1	donner	1
acheter	1	commencer	1	dresser	1
additionner	1	communiquer	1	durer	1
adorer	1	compatir	2		
adoucir	2	compter	1	échanger	1
agrandir	2	concerner	1	échouer à	1
aimer	1	confier	1	économiser	1
amener	1	confirmer	1	écouter	1
anéantir	2	confondre	3	éliminer	1
annoncer	1	consacrer	1	éluder	1
annuler	1	conseiller	1	emménager	1
appeler	1	considérer	1	emmener	1
applaudir	2	consister à	1	empêcher	1
apporter	1	contacter	1	empirer	1
approfondir	2	coordonner	1	employer	1
arranger	1	coordiner	1	emprunter	1
arrêter	1	couper	1	encourager	1
arriver	1*	coûter	1	enfermer	1
assister à	1	créer	1	engager	1
assurer	1	cultiver	1	enlever	1
attacher	1			ennuyer	1
attendre	3	déborder	1	énoncer	1
atterrir	2	débuter	1	enregistrer	1
attirer	1	décider	1	enseigner	1
avertir	2	décourager	1	entamer	1
		décrocher	1	entendre	3
baisser	1	dégoûter	1	entraîner	1
bénéficier de	1	déjeuner	1	entrer	1*
bouger	1	délaisser	1	envisager	1
bouleverser	1	demander	1	envoyer	1
bronzer	1	démarrer	1	épargner	1
		déménager	1	épeler	1
cacher	1	dépenser	1	épuiser	1
caler	1	déplacer	1	espérer	1
calmer	1	déposer	1	essayer	1
caser	1	déranger	1	estimer	1
casser	1	descendre	3**	établir	2
centraliser	1	désirer	1	étonner	1
changer	1	destiner	1	étouffer	1
chauffer	1	détester	1	étudier	1
chercher	1			éviter	1

évoquer	1	jeter	1	procéder	1
exagérer	1	jouer	1	profiter de	1
examiner	1			progresser	1
exciter	1	laisser	1	proposer	1
excuser	1	libérer	1	prouver	1
exercer	1	loger	1		
exiger	1	lutter	1	questionner	1
exister	1			quitter	1
expédier	1	manquer	1		
expliquer	1	marcher	1	raccompagner	1
exploiter	1	mener	1	raccrocher	1
exposer	1	mentionner	1	raconter	1
exprimer	1	monter	1**	rajouter	1
		montrer	1	ranger	1
fabriquer	1			rappeler	1
faciliter	1	négliger	1	rapporter	1
féliciter	1	noter	1	rassurer	1
fermer	1			réaliser	1
finir	1	obéir	2	récapituler	1
fixer	1	obliger	1	rechercher	1
flatter	1	occuper	1	récolter	1
flécher	1	organiser	1	recommencer	1
fonctionner	1	oublier	1	rectifier	1
former	1			récupérer	1
fournir	2	parier	1	rédiger	1
fréquenter	1	parler	1	réécouter	1
froisser	1	parrainer	1	réentendre	3
fumer	1	partager	1	réfléchir	2
		participer à	1	refuser	1
gagner	1	passer	1**	regarder	1
garder	1	patienter	1	régler	1
garer	1	patronner	1	regretter	1
gaspiller	1	payer	1	rehausser	1
gâter	1	penser	1	remarquer	1
gémir	2	perdre	3	rembourser	1
goûter	1	persuader	1	remplacer	1
		photocopier	1	remplir	2
habiter	1	pique-niquer	1	rencontrer	1
héberger	1	placer	1	rendre	3
		plaisanter	1	renouveler	1
illustrer	1	pleurer	1	rentrer	1*
imaginer	1	porter	1	repérer	1
indiquer	1	poser	1	répéter	1
insister	1	posséder	1	répondre	3
intéresser	1	préférer	1	réserver	1
interrompre	3	préparer	1	résister	1
interviewer	1	présenter	1	ressembler à	1
inventer	1	presser	1	rester	1
inviter	1	prêter	1	résulter	1**
		prier	1	retourner	1*

rétrécir	2	soumissionner	1	tourner	1
retrouver	1	soutirer	1	traiter	1
réussir à	2	suggérer	1	transporter	1
réveiller	1	supplier	1	travailler	1
réviser	1	supposer	1	traverser	1
risquer de	1	supprimer	1	trouver	1
rouler	1	surprendre	3		
ruminer	1			utiliser	1
		tâcher de	1		
saisir	2	taper	1	vendre	3
sélectionner	1	tarder	1	vérifier	1
sembler	1	téléphoner	1	vexer	1
signer	1	terminer	1	vider	1
signifier	1	tirer	1	visiter	1
songer à	1	tomber	1*	voyager	1
souhaiter	1	toucher	1		

1, 2, 3 = Group to which verb belongs. Conjugated with **avoir**
unless marked.
* Verb conjugated with **être** in the past tenses.
** Verb conjugated with **avoir** or **être** in the past tenses.
The choice depends on whether the verb is transitive (takes
an object) or intransitive. For example, **descendre:**

> **J'ai descendu l'escalier en courant.**
> (Transitive, so **avoir**)
> **Je suis descendu très vite.**
> (Intransitive, so **être**)

13 Four common irregular verbs: être, avoir, aller, faire

être

Present	Imperfect	Future
je suis	j'étais	je serai
tu es	tu étais	tu seras
il	il	il
elle est	elle était	elle sera
nous sommes	nous étions	nous serons
vous êtes	vous étiez	vous serez
ils	ils	ils
elles sont	elles étaient	elles seront

Future Perfect	Present Perfect	Pluperfect
j'aurai été	j'ai été	j'avais été
tu auras été	tu as été	tu avais été
il	il	il
elle aura été	elle a été	elle avait été
nous aurons été	nous avons été	nous avions été
vous aurez été	vous avez été	vous aviez été
ils	ils	ils
elles auront été	elles ont été	elles avaient été

Conditional	Past Conditional	Subjunctive
je serais	j'aurais été	que je sois
tu serais	tu aurais été	que tu sois
il	il	qu'il
elle serait	elle aurait été	qu'elle soit
nous serions	nous aurions été	que nous soyons
vous seriez	vous auriez été	que vous soyez
ils	ils	qu'ils
elles seraient	elles auraient été	qu'elles soient

Imperative: **sois   soyons   soyez**

avoir

Present	Imperfect	Future
j'ai	j'avais	j'aurai
tu as	tu avais	tu auras
il	il	il
elle a	elle avait	elle aura
nous avons	nous avions	nous aurons
vous avez	vous aviez	vous aurez
ils	ils	ils
elles ont	elles avaient	elles auront

Future Perfect	Present Perfect	Pluperfect
j'aurai eu	j'ai eu	j'avais eu
tu auras eu	tu as eu	tu avais eu
il	il	il
elle aura eu	elle a eu	elle avait eu
nous aurons eu	nous avons eu	nous avions eu
vous aurez eu	vous avez eu	vous aviez eu
ils	ils	ils
elles auront eu	elles ont eu	elles avaient eu

Conditional	Past Conditional	Subjunctive
j'aurais	j'aurais eu	que j'aie
tu aurais	tu aurais eu	que tu aies
Il	il	qu'il
elle aurait	elle aurait eu	qu'elle ait
nous aurions	nous aurions eu	que nous ayons
vous auriez	vous auriez eu	que vous ayez
ils	ils	qu'ils
elles auraient	elles auraient eu	qu'elles aient

Imperative: **aie   ayons   ayez**

aller

Present	Imperfect	Future
je vais	j'allais	j'irai
tu vas	tu allais	tu iras
il	il	il
elle va	elle allait	elle ira
nous allons	nous allions	nous irons
vous allez	vous alliez	vous irez
ils	ils	ils
elles vont	elles allaient	elles iront

Future Perfect	Present Perfect	Pluperfect
je serai allé/e	je suis allé/e	j'étais allé/e
tu seras allé/e	tu es allé/e	tu étais allé/e
il sera allé	il est allé	il était allé
elle sera allée	elle est allée	elle était allée
nous serons allés/ées	nous sommes allés/ ées	nous étions allés/ées
vous serez allés/ées	vous êtes allés/ées	vous étiez allés/ées
ils seront allés	ils sont allés	ils étaient allés
elles seront allées	elles sont allées	elles étaient allées

Conditional	Past Conditional	Subjunctive
j'irais	je serais allé/e	que j'aille
tu irais	tu serais allé/e	que tu ailles
il	il serait allé	qu'il aille
elle irait	elle serait allée	qu'elle aille
nous irions	nous serions allés/ ées	que nous allions
vous iriez	vous seriez allés/ées	que vous alliez
ils	ils seraient allés	qu'ils
elles iraient	elles seraient allées	qu'elles aillent

Imperative: **va**   **allons**   **allez**

faire

Present	Imperfect	Future
je fais	je faisais	je ferai
tu fais	tu faisais	tu feras
il elle **fait**	il elle **faisait**	il elle **fera**
nous faisons	nous faisions	nous ferons
vous faites	vous faisiez	vous ferez
ils elles **font**	ils elles **faisaient**	ils elles **feront**

Future Perfect	Present Perfect	Pluperfect
j'aurai fait	j'ai fait	j'avais fait
tu auras fait	tu as fait	tu avais fait
il elle **aura fait**	il elle **a fait**	il elle **avait fait**
nous aurons fait	nous avons fait	nous avions fait
vous aurez fait	vous avez fait	vous aviez fait
ils elles **auront fait**	ils elles **ont fait**	ils elles **avaient fait**

Conditional	Past Conditional	Subjunctive
je ferais	j'aurais fait	que je fasse
tu ferais	tu aurais fait	que tu fasses
il elle **ferait**	il elle **aurait fait**	qu'il qu'elle **fasse**
nous ferions	nous aurions fait	que nous fassions
vous feriez	vous auriez fait	que vous fassiez
ils elles **feraient**	ils elles **auraient fait**	qu'ils qu'elles **fassent**

Imperative: **fais   faisons   faites**

14 Irregular verbs in the course

Verb	Present Participle	Present	Future	Subjunctive	Imperative	Past Participle	Auxiliary
accueillir	accueillant	j'accueille tu accueilles il accueille nous accueillons vous accueillez ils accueillent	j'accueillerai	que j'accueille	accueille accueillons accueillez	accueilli	avoir
acquérir	acquérant	j'acquiers il acquiert nous acquérons ils acquièrent	j'acquerrai	que j'acquière	acquiers acquérons acquérez	acquis	avoir
apparaître (see paraître) appartenir (see tenir) apprendre (see prendre)							
boire	buvant	je bois il boit nous buvons ils boivent	je boirai	que je boive	bois buvons buvez	bu	avoir
bouillir	bouillant	je bous il bout nous bouillons ils bouillent	je bouillirai	que je bouille	not used	bouilli	avoir
comprendre (see prendre)							

Infinitive	Participle	Present	Future	Subjunctive	Imperative	Past Part.	Aux.
conduire	conduisant	je conduis il conduit nous conduisons ils conduisent	je conduirai	que je conduise	conduis conduisons conduisez	conduit	avoir
connaître	connaissant	je connais il connaît nous connaissons ils connaissent	je connaîtrai	que je connaisse	connais connaissons connaissez	connu	avoir
contredire (See dire)							
convaincre	convainquant	je convaincs il convainc nous convainquons ils convainquent	je convaincrai	que je convainque	convaincs convainquons convainquez	convaincu	avoir
convenir (see venir)							
croire	croyant	je crois il croit nous croyons ils croient	je croirai	que je croie	crois croyons croyez	cru	avoir
découvrir (see ouvrir) décrire (see écrire) déplaire (see plaire) détenir (see tenir) devenir (see venir)							
devoir	devant	je dois il doit nous devons ils doivent	je devrai	que je doive	not used	dû	avoir

Verb	Present Participle	Present	Future	Subjunctive	Imperative	Past Participle	Auxiliary
dire	disant	je dis tu dis il dit nous disons vous dites ils disent	je dirai	que je dise	dis disons dites	dit	avoir
dormir	dormant	je dors il dort nous dormons ils dorment	je dormirai	que je dorme	dors dormons dormez	dormi	avoir
écrire	écrivant	j'écris il écrit nous écrivons ils écrivent	j'écrirai	que j'écrive	écris écrivons écrivez	écrit	avoir
éteindre	éteignant	j'éteins il éteint nous éteignons ils éteignent	j'éteindrai	que j'éteigne	éteins éteignons éteignez	éteint	avoir
faillir	faillant	not used – this verb is used only in the Perfect & Future tenses	je faillirai			failli (j'ai failli)	avoir
falloir impersonal		il faut	il faudra	qu'il faille		fallu	avoir

inscrire (see écrire)

intervenir (see venir)

jeter	jetant	je jette il jette nous jetons ils jettent	je jetterai	que je jette	jette jetons jetez	jeté	avoir
joindre	joignant	je joins il joint nous joignons ils joignent	je joindrai	que je joigne	joins joignons joignez	joint	avoir
lire	lisant	je lis il lit nous lisons ils lisent	je lirai	que je lise	lis lisons lisez	lu	avoir
mentir	mentant	je mens il ment nous mentons ils mentent	je mentirai	que je mente	mens mentons mentez	menti	avoir
mettre	mettant	je mets il met nous mettons ils mettent	je mettrai	que je mette	mets mettons mettez	mis	avoir
naître	naissant	je nais il naît nous naissons ils naissent	je naîtrai	que je naisse	not used	né	être

obtenir (see tenir)

Verb	Present Participle	Present	Future	Subjunctive	Imperative	Past Participle	Auxiliary
offrir	offrant	j'offre il offre nous offrons ils offrent	j'offrirai	que j'offre	offre offrons offrez	offert	avoir
ouvrir	ouvrant	j'ouvre il ouvre nous ouvrons ils ouvrent	j'ouvrirai	que j'ouvre	ouvre ouvrons ouvrez	ouvert	avoir
paraître	paraissant	je parais il paraît nous paraissons ils paraissent	je paraîtrai	que je paraisse	parais paraissons paraissez	paru	avoir
partir	partant	je pars il part nous partons ils partent	je partirai	que je parte	pars partons partez	parti	être
permettre (see mettre)							
plaire	plaisant	je plais il plaît nous plaisons ils plaisent	je plairai	que je plaise	plais plaisons plaisez	plu	avoir
poursuivre (see suivre)							

pouvoir	pouvant	je peux il peut nous pouvons ils peuvent	je pourrai	que je puisse	not used	pu	avoir
prendre	prenant	je prends il prend nous prenons ils prennent	je prendrai	que je prenne	prends prenons prenez	pris	avoir
prévenir (see venir) prévoir (see voir) promettre (see mettre)							
recevoir	recevant	je reçois il reçoit nous recevons ils reçoivent	je recevrai	que je reçoive	reçois recevons recevez	reçu	avoir
rejoindre (see joindre) reprendre (see prendre)							
ressentir	ressentant	je ressens il ressent nous ressentons ils ressentent	je ressentirai	que je ressente	ressens ressentons ressentez	ressenti	avoir
revenir (see venir)							
rire	riant	je ris il rit nous rions ils rient	je rirai	que je rie	ris rions riez	ri	avoir

Verb	Present Participle	Present	Future	Subjunctive	Imperative	Past Participle	Auxiliary
rompre	rompant	je romps il rompt nous rompons ils rompent	je romprai	que je romps	romps rompons rompez	rompu	avoir
savoir	sachant	je sais il sait nous savons ils savent	je saurai	que je sache	sache sachons sachez	su	avoir
servir	servant	je sers il sert nous servons ils servent	je servirai	que je serve	sers servons servez	servi	avoir
sortir	sortant	je sors il sort nous sortons ils sortent	je sortirai	que je sorte	sors sortons sortez	sorti	être
soumettre (see mettre) soutenir (see tenir)							
suffire	suffisant	je suffis il suffit nous suffisons ils suffisent	je suffirai	que je suffise	suffis suffisons suffisez	suffi	avoir
suivre	suivant	je suis il suit nous suivons ils suivent	je suivrai	que je suive	suis suivons suivez	suivi	avoir

Infinitive	Present participle	Present	Future	Subjunctive	Imperative	Past participle	Auxiliary
tenir	tenant	je tiens il tient nous tenons ils tiennent	je tiendrai	que je tienne	tiens tenons tenez	tenu	avoir
transmettre (see mettre)							
valoir	valant	je vaux il vaut nous valons ils valent	je vaudrai	que je vaille (que nous valions) qu'ils valent)	not used	valu	avoir
venir	venant	je viens il vient nous venons ils viennent	je viendrai	que je vienne	viens venons venez	venu	être
vivre	vivant	je vis il vit nous vivons ils vivent	je vivrai	que je vive	vis vivons vivez	vécu	avoir
voir	voyant	je vois il voit nous voyons ils voient	je verrai	que je voie	vois voyons voyez	vu	avoir
vouloir	voulant	je veux il veut nous voulons ils veulent	je voudrai	que je veuille que nous voulions	veuille (nous form not used) veuillez	voulu	avoir

15   Reflexive verbs

Regular reflexives

All conjugated with **être** in the past (compound) tenses.

s'absenter (1)
s'achever (1)
s'adresser à (1)
s'agir de (2)
s'agrandir (2)
s'aider (1)
s'allumer (1)
s'amuser (1)
s'appeler (1)
s'arranger (1)
s'arrêter (1)
s'assurer (1)
s'attirer (1)

se battre (3)

se calmer (1)
se changer (1)
se consoler (1)
se contenter de (1)
se coucher (1)
se croire (3)

se débrouiller (1)
se décider (1)
se demander (1)
se dépêcher (1)
se déplacer (1)
se dérouler (1)
se détendre (1)

s'échauffer (1)
s'empêcher de (1)
s'enfoncer (1)
s'engager (1)
s'ennuyer (1)
s'entendre (3)
s'entraider (1)
s'entraîner (1)
s'établir (2)
s'excuser (1)
s'exercer (1)

se fâcher (1)
se familiariser (1)

s'habituer (1)

s'inquiéter (1)
s'installer (1)
s'intégrer (1)

se lasser (1)
se laver (1)
se lever (1)
se libérer (1)
se loger (1)

se marier (1)
se mêler de (1)
se monter à (1)

s'occuper (1)
s'organiser (1)

se parler (1)
se passer (1)
se pencher (1)
se préparer (1)
se présenter (1)
se promener (1)

se rafraîchir (2)
se rappeler (1)
se raser (1)
se rassurer (1)
se reculer (1)
se relaxer (1)
se rencontrer (1)
se renseigner (1)
se reposer (1)
se retrouver (1)
se réunir (2)
se réveiller (1)

se séparer (1)

se tromper (1)
se trouver (1)

Irregular reflexive verbs

Verb	Present Participle	Present	Future	Subjunctive	Imperative	Past Participle	Auxiliary
s'asseoir	s'asseyant	je m'asseois/m'assieds il s'asseoit/s'assied nous nous asseyons ils s'asseoient/s'asseyent	je m'assiérai	que je m'asseoie/ m'asseye	assieds-toi asseyons-nous asseyez-vous	assis	être
s'y connaître (see connaître)							être
s'écrire (see écrire)							être
s'éteindre (see éteindre)							être
se faire (see faire)							être
se plaindre	se plaignant	je me plains il se plaint nous nous plaignons ils se plaignent	je me plaindrai	que je me plaigne	plains-toi plaignons-nous plaignez-vous	plaint	être
se prendre (see prendre)							
se remettre (see mettre)							
se rendre	se rendant	je me rends il se rend nous nous rendons ils se rendent	je me rendrai	que je me rende	rends-toi rendons-nous rendez-vous	rendu	être
se sentir	se sentant	je me sens il se sent nous nous sentons ils se sentent	je me sentirai	que je me sente	sens-toi sentons-nous sentez-vous	senti	être
s'en sortir (see sortir)							
se souvenir (see venir)							

16   The passive

The passive is used less frequently in French than in English, the **on** form often being used instead. Remember, of course, that only transitive verbs have a passive form. The passive of all verbs is formed with **être,** and the past participle must therefore agree with the subject.
Some examples:

Didier n'est pas convaincu.
Didier isn't convinced.
Delphine n'était pas convaincue.
Delphine wasn't convinced.
Didier et Delphine ne sont pas convaincus.
Didier and Delphine aren't convinced.
Je ne serai pas convaincu.
I will not be convinced.

17   Expressions followed by the subjunctive

CONJUNCTIONS

à moins que
avant que
bien que
à condition que
le temps que
pour que

VERBS

attendre que
craindre que
souhaiter que
vouloir que

VERBAL PHRASES

aimer bien que
s'arranger pour que
avoir peur que ... ne

ça ne vous dérange pas que ...?
c'est dommage que
c'est mieux que

être content que
être désolé que

faire en sorte que

il faut que
il faudra que
il va falloir que

il se peut que
il est préférable que

il suffit que

il est temps que

vous permettez que

18   Verbs and phrases followed by:
à or de + Infinitive

Verbs + à + Infinitive   Verbal phrases + à

apprendre à	**inviter à**	**avoir beaucoup de choses à**
arriver à		**n'avoir qu'à**
avoir à	**penser à**	**avoir du mal à**
	pousser à	
chercher à	**se préparer à**	**ne demander qu'à**
commencer à		
consister à	**réussir à**	**être trop occupé à**
continuer à		**être prêt à**
	servir à	
se décider à	**songer à**	**voir un inconvénient à**
demander à		
	tarder à	
s'exercer à	**tenir à**	

Verbs + de + Infinitive

ne pas arrêter de	**s'occuper de**
décider de	**parler de (faire quelque chose)**
demander de	**permettre de**
dire de	**prier de**
s'efforcer de	**refuser de**
empêcher de	**remercier de**
s'empêcher de	
essayer de	**suggérer de**
s'excuser de	**supplier de**
finir de	**tâcher de**

Verbal phrases + de

il s'agit de
c'est agréable de
ça a l'air de
en avoir assez de
avoir besoin de
avoir envie de
avoir l'intention de
avoir des chances de
avoir pour but de
avoir pour objectif de

c'est à cent lieux de
il est conseillé de
ça coûte une fortune de

ça me déplaît de
ça vous dérangerait de?
c'est plus difficile de
c'est dommage de

ça m'est égal de
être capable de
être chargé de
être content de
être curieux de
être désolé de
être heureux de
être prié de
être sûr de
être en train de

c'est facile de
faire bien de

c'est gentil à vous de

il est l'heure de
c'est plus honnête de

c'est une bonne idée de
il est important de
ça l'intéresse de
il est inutile de

être en mesure de
on ferait mieux de
avoir les moyens de

il est nécessaire de

avoir l'occasion de

ce n'est pas la peine de
ça te plairait de
ça fait plaisir de
il y a toujours la possibilité de
il est possible (à quelqu'un) de
ne pas pouvoir s'empêcher de
il est prudent de

il est question de

avoir des raisons de
être ravi de
ça risque de

avoir le temps de
il est temps de
c'est ton tour de

c'est utile de

GLOSSARY OF
GRAMMATICAL TERMS

Glossary of Grammatical Terms

ADJECTIVE: word added to a noun to describe it more fully: **une petite maison:** *a small house* – **petite** is an adjective.

ADVERB: word which modifies, defines more precisely the meaning of an adjective, a verb, or another adverb. It can give details of time, place, manner: **une maison *vraiment* petite, marcher *doucement*, parler *trop* fort,** etc.

ARTICLE: small word which always accompanies the noun and indicates its gender: **le/la/les** *(the)* is the definite article; **un/une/des** *(a, some)* is the indefinite article.

CLAUSE: short sentence, inside a longer one. For instance: **Je ne sais pas** is the main clause, **ce qu'elle a dit** is the subordinate clause, depending on the main one, and **Je ne sais pas ce qu'elle a dit** is the sentence.

COMPOUND TENSE: a tense in which the verb includes two parts: the auxiliary (**avoir** or **être**) and the Past Participle of the verb being conjugated. For instance:

Perfect tense	**Je suis allé**	
Pluperfect	**Il était allé**	All these are
Future Perfect	**Il sera allé**	compound tenses.
Past Conditional	**Il serait allé**	

CONJUNCTION: small word used to connect clauses or sentences; **mais, ou, et, donc, or, ni, car** are used to link sentences, **pour que, afin que, avant que,** are used to link two clauses.

DEMONSTRATIVE: demonstrative adjectives or pronouns are used to point out things or people: **ce livre, celui-ci.**

DIRECT OBJECT COMPLEMENT: noun or pronoun affected by the action of the verb, and linked to the verb directly, without the need to use a preposition such as **à**: **Je mange *un gâteau*, Je connais *le professeur*.**

DIRECT OBJECT PRONOUN: pronoun used as direct object complement, answering the questions **qui est-ce que?** and **qu'est-ce que?**: **Je *le* vois, Je *la* connais, Je *les* mange.**

DIRECT SPEECH: words quoted directly, not reported by someone else, without the need to use expressions such as **il a dit que, elle a demandé si,** etc.

EMPHATIC CONSTRUCTION: sentence structure used to stress a particular word or group of words in the sentence.

INDIRECT OBJECT COMPLEMENT: noun or pronoun affected by
the action of the verb, but indirectly linked to the verb
through the use of a preposition, such as **à:**
Je donne un livre à Pierre:
à Pierre is the indirect object complement
Je lui donne un livre:
lui *(= to him)* is the indirect object, **un livre** being the
direct object complement.
INFINITIVE: this is the form of the verb which just gives its
name, without the verb being conjugated: **aimer, finir,
aller, jouer, comprendre** are infinitives.
INTERROGATIVE: interrogative adjectives and pronouns are
used to ask a question. For instance: *Qui* **est-ce?** *Quel*
livre voulez-vous? *Lesquels* **connaissez-vous?**
INTRANSITIVE VERB: this is a verb which cannot have a direct
object complement. For instance **aller.** Intransitive verbs
are conjugated with **être** in the Perfect and other
compound tenses.
INVERSION OF SUBJECT: this refers to a construction in which
the verb comes first and the subject in second place. For
instance: **Voulez-vous? Veux-tu?**
PARTICIPLE: two kinds of participles:
Present Participle: **aimant, jouant, allant,** etc.
Past Participle: **aimé, joué, allé, fini,** etc.
The Past Participle is used to conjugate the verb in a
compound tense, such as the Perfect tense: **je suis allé, j'ai
joué** or the Pluperfect: **j'étais allé, j'avais joué,**etc.
Both types of participle can be used as adjectives: **un
enfant très aimé** *(a very well-loved child);* **un enfant très
aimant** *(a very loving child).*
POSSESSIVE: possessive adjectives and pronouns indicate a
relation of possession between people or things:
mon **père** *(my father); le mien (mine).*
PREPOSITION: a small word, invariable, which links two words
or groups of words. For instance: **pour, avec, par, sur,
sous, à, de** are prepositions.
PRONOUN: a pronoun is used to replace a noun. It can be
the subject or object of the verb. **Pierre joue.** *Il*
joue. Jean joue avec Pierre. Jean joue avec *lui.*

REPORTED SPEECH: someone's words are reported, repeated by another person, with the help of expressions such as **il a dit que/elle a demandé si/ils ont dit que,** etc.

SUBJECT: is the noun or pronoun which performs the action described by the verb, or which is in the state described by the verb, or which "suffers" the action described by the verb: **Pierre mange une pomme.**

Elle est fatiguée.

Ils ont reçu une lettre hier.

SUBORDINATE CLAUSE: a clause which depends on another clause in the sentence, and to which it is linked by a relative pronoun or a conjunction. See CLAUSE.

TRANSITIVE VERB: a verb which takes a direct object complement. For instance **manger, boire, dire, sauter, finir** are transitive verbs. For example:

Ils mangent un steak.

VERB: word which in the sentence describes an action or a state performed or suffered by the subject.

Je *donne* **des lettres à ma secrétaire.**

Les étudiants *paraissent* **très fatigués.**

ALPHABETICAL VOCABULARY

Alphabetical vocabulary

là-dessus *4.1.S5*
laisser *1.1.S2*
lancer *2.2.S1*
langue *2.2.S2*
lendemain *2.2.E5*
lentement *1.2.E3*
lequel *4.1.S1*
lettre *3.1.S4*
lever *2.2.E5*
se libérer *4.2.S2*
libre 3.1.S2
lieu *4.2.E1*
au lieu de *1.2.E4*
ligne *4.2.E1*
à la ligne *2.1.S6*
en ligne *4.1.S6*
en liquide *1.2.S5*
lit *2.2.S5*
livraison *3.2.S6*
locataire *2.1.S1*
locomotive *1.2.S6*
logement *2.1.S3*
se loger *4.2.E3*
loi *4.1.S1*
longtemps *4.1.S4*
lot *3.2.S4*
louche *4.1.S1*
loyer *2.1.S1*

M

machine à écrire *2.1.E2*
magnétique *3.2.S4*
main d'œuvre *4.1.S5*
se maintenir *3.1.S2*
maison *2.2.S2*
majuscule *1.1.E2*
mal *4.1.S3*
malade *4.2.S5*
malentendu *2.1.S4*
malheureusement *3.2.S4*
manière *2.1.E4*

manquer *1.1.S5, 1.2.S1*
marcher *2.2.S3*
se marier *2.2.S3*
marketing *2.1.E5*
matériel *1.2.S6*
matin *2.2.E5*
meilleur *3.1.S6*
même *1.2.S3*
mener *4.1.S6*
mener à bien *3.1.S4*
mensuel *3.1.E4*
mesquin *2.2.S4*
en mesure de *4.1.S5*
métier *4.2.S3*
mètres carrés *2.1.S1*
mettre au point *1.2.S6*
mettre en place *2.1.S6*
se mettre à *2.1.S3*
mi-temps *4.2.E3*
mien, le mien, la mienne
    1.1.E3
mieux *1.2.E4*
milieu *1.2.S6, 4.2.E1*
mince *3.1.S5*
minuscule *4.1.S2*
minutage *3.2.S4*
à la mode (de)*2.2.E3*
le moindre *4.2.S2*
au moins *1.2.S3*
en moins *3.2.S1*
moment *1.2.S4*
du moment que *3.1.E4*
monde *4.1.S5*
se monter (à) *2.1.E1*
moteur *3.2.S4*
mouvementé *2.1.S6*
moyen *1.1.S6*
Moyen-Orient *1.2.S6*
moyens de transport *3.2.S6*
muni (de) *1.2.S6*
muter *2.2.S2*

N
naître *3.2.S4*
navré *1.1.E5*
ne ... plus *3.1.S1*
ne ... que *3.1.S1*
niveau *2.1.S6*
nombreux *3.1.S4*
non plus *1.1.S6*
nouveau *2.2.S6*
à nouveau *3.1.S2*
nouvelle(s) *1.1.S3*
nuit *4.1.S3*
numéro *2.1.S2*

O
obtenir *3.2.S6*
occasion *3.1.S2*
occasionné *4.1.S5*
occupé *2.1.E3*
s'occuper (de) *1.1.S5*
offre publique *4.1.S1*
ordinateur *2.1.S2*
ordre *1.2.S5, 4.2.E2*
ordre du jour *3.2.S5*
ouvert *1.2.E5*
ouvrir *1.1.S2*

P
en panne *1.2.E1*
par conséquent *1.2.E2*
pareil *3.1.S1*
parier *3.1.S4*
parole *3.1.S2*
d'autre part *2.2.S4*
de la part de *1.2.S1*
participer *4.1.E1*
partir *1.1.S6*
à partir de *2.2.S4*
partout *1.1.E5*
parvenir (à) *2.1.S6, 4.1.S1*
pas mal de *1.2.E5*

passager *4.2.S6*
passer *3.1.E4, 4.1.S6*
se passer *1.1.S4*
passionnant *1.1.S5*
patron *4.1.S4*
peine *3.1.S1*
pendant *2.2.S3*
pendule *3.2.E3*
pénible *3.1.S5*
penser *1.2.S1*
perdu *3.1.S1*
permettre *1.1.E1*
en personne *4.2.S2*
personnel *2.1.S3*
perte *2.2.S6*
peste *2.1.S5*
peu importe *2.2.S3*
il se peut que *1.2.S6*
philosophe *4.2.E5*
photocopier *4.1.S1*
photocopieuse *2.1.S2*
pièce *1.2.S1*
pire *3.1.S5*
placard *3.2.E2*
place *4.1.S5*
se plaindre *2.2.S6*
plaire *1.1.S5*
plaisanter *1.1.S3*
planification *3.2.S6*
planning *2.2.E1*
la plupart (de) *2.2.S2*
plus ... que *2.1.S6*
plutôt *2.2.S4*
pneumatique *3.2.S4*
poids *3.2.S1*
point *2.1.S6, 4.2.S1*
à point *4.1.E2*
au point *4.2.S2*
point d'interrogation *4.2.S1*
point de vue *4.1.S5*
de pointe *3.1.S2*

LANGUAGE AND TRAVEL BOOKS
FROM PASSPORT BOOKS

Dictionaries and References
Spanish and English Dictionaries
Harrap's Concise Spanish and English
Dictionary
Harrap's French and English Dictionaries
Harrap German and English Dictionary
Harrap's Concise German and English
Dictionary
Everyday American English Dictionary
Beginner's Dictionary of American
English Usage
Diccionario Inglés
El Diccionario del Español Chicano
Diccionario Básico Norteamericano
British/American Language Dictionary
The French Businessmate
The German Businessmate
The Spanish Businessmate
Harrap's Slang Dictionary (French and English)
English Picture Dictionary
French Picture Dictionary
Spanish Picture Dictionary
German Picture Dictionary
Guide to Spanish Idioms
Guide to German Idioms
Guide to French Idioms
Guide to Correspondence in Spanish
Guide to Correspondence in French
Español para los Hispanos
Business Russian
Yes! You Can Learn a Foreign Language
Everyday Japanese
Japanese in Plain English
Korean in Plain English
Robin Hyman's Dictionary of Quotations
NTC's American Idioms Dictionary
Passport's Japan Almanac
Japanese Etiquette and Ethics in
Business
How To Do Business With The Japanese
Korean Etiquette And Ethics In Business

Verb References
Complete Handbook of Spanish Verbs
Spanish Verb Drills
French Verb Drills
German Verb Drills

Grammar References
Spanish Verbs and Essentials of Grammar
Nice 'n Easy Spanish Grammar
French Verbs and Essentials of Grammar
Nice 'n Easy French Grammar
German Verbs and Essentials of Grammar
Nice 'n Easy German Grammar
Italian Verbs and Essentials of Grammar
Essentials of Russian Grammar

Welcome Books
Welcome to Spain
Welcome to France
Welcome to Ancient Greece
Welcome to Ancient Rome

Language Programs
Just Listen 'n Learn: Spanish, French, Italian,
German and Greek
Just Listen 'n Learn Plus: Spanish, French,
and German
Practice & Improve Your . . . Spanish, French
and German
Practice & Improve Your . . . Spanish, French and
German PLUS
Japanese For Children
Basic French Conversation
Basic Spanish Conversation

Phrase Books
Just Enough Dutch
Just Enough French
Just Enough German
Just Enough Greek
Just Enough Italian
Just Enough Japanese
Just Enough Portuguese
Just Enough Scandinavian
Just Enough Serbo-Croat
Just Enough Spanish
Multilingual Phrase Book
International Traveler's Phrasebook

Language Game Books
Easy French Crossword Puzzles
Easy French Word Games and Puzzles
Easy Spanish Crossword Puzzles
Easy Spanish Word Games and Puzzles
Let's Learn About Series: Italy, France,
Germany, Spain, America
Let's Learn Coloring Books In Spanish,
French, German, Italian, And English

Humor in Five Languages
The Insult Dictionary: How to Give 'Em
Hell in 5 Nasty Languages
The Lover's Dictionary: How to Be
Amorous in 5 Delectable Languages

Technical Dictionaries
Complete Multilingual Dictionary of
Computer Terminology
Complete Multilingual Dictionary of
Aviation and Aeronautical Terminology
Complete Multilingual Dictionary of
Advertising, Marketing and Communications
Harrap's French and English
Business Dictionary
Harrap's French and English
Science Dictionary

Travel
Nagel's Encyclopedia Guides
World at Its Best Travel Series
Runaway Travel Guides
Mystery Reader's Walking Guide: London
Japan Today
Japan at Night
Discovering Cultural Japan
Bon Voyage!
Business Capitals of the World
Hiking and Walking Guide to Europe
Frequent Flyer's Award Book
Ethnic London
European Atlas
Health Guide for International Travelers
Passport's Travel Paks: Britain, Italy,
France, Germany, Spain
Passport's China Guides
On Your Own Series: Brazil, Israel
Spain Under the Sun Series: Barcelona, Toledo,
Seville and Marbella

Getting Started Books
Introductory language books for Spanish,
French, German and Italian.

For Beginners Series
Introductory language books for children
in Spanish, French, German and Italian.

PASSPORT BOOKS
a division of NTC *Publishing Group*
4255 West Touhy Avenue
Lincolnwood, Illinois 60646-1975